7 THINGS KIDS NEVER FORGET

7 THINGS KIDS NEVER FORGET

And How to Make the Most of Them

RON ROSE

SEVEN THINGS KIDS NEVER FORGET

published by Multnomah Books
a part of the Questar publishing family

© 1993 by Ron Rose

International Standard Book Number: 0945564-79-1

Printed in the United States of America

Scripture quotations are from The *New American Standard Bible*
© 1960, 1977 by the Lockman Foundation; used by permission

Library of Congress Cataloging-in-Publication Data
Rose, Ron.   Seven things kids never forget/by Ron Rose
p.cm   Includes bibliographical references.   ISBN 0-945564-79-1
1. Parent and child. 2. Communication in the family. 3. Parenting. I. Title
HQ755.85.R657   1993   93-29226
306.874--dc20   CIP

For information:
QUESTAR PUBLISHERS, INC.
POST OFFICE BOX 1720
SISTERS, OREGON 97759

94 95 96 97 98 99 00 01 — 10 9 8 7 6 5 4 3 2

DEDICATION

To my wife, Lyn, my companion for life,
who is always ready to make a new memory.

To my parents, John and Thelma,
who shaped the story of my childhood
and beyond.

To my girls, Julie and Joy,
who are still writing the sequel.

Thanks for the memories.

CONTENTS

Chapter One

MAKING MOMENTS INTO MEMORIES

The poignant chorus of a Gaither song tugs at my heartstrings: "We have these moments to hold in our hands and to touch as they slip through our fingers like sand. Yesterday's gone and tomorrow may never come, but we have these moments today."[1]

This book is filled with moments that have become memories, but it is far more than a pursuit of nostalgia. This book contains the memories of multiple generations. Its purpose is to put parent education into the context of life. And its prayer is to offer hope to parents, to give a taste of possibility in an impossible world.

WHAT MAKES A MEMORY?

We are all memory collectors, although at times we're not sure where we put the collection. And our stash of memories is unique. Even though two people may experience the same event, their memories of it will be different. For example, a youngster may attend a historic baseball no-hitter but only remember the hot dog he bought from the vendor. That's just the way we're made.

Our memory is not like computer memory. After we experience an event, we rarely recall the story exactly as it happened. Once something enters our brain, it's colored by our expectations, our view of life, our past, our interpretations, and our values. That's why much of the new, bullet-filled, "fast read" writing style is so frustrating to searching parents. Bullets don't have emotion, they don't have context, and they assume everyone fits the same mold. Memories are not made with bulleted lists. Memories are generated by events and emotions.

Arthur Gordon, a past editorial director for *Guideposts*, tells wonderful stories about real people and their memories. One of my favorites captures a conversation between a father and daughter the night before her wedding, and it illustrates why memory making within families is so important.

> They sat together on the porch steps, so close that their moon shadow was a single wedge of blackness against the weathered wood. Tomorrow was the wedding, with all the excitement and confusion, tears and laughter....
>
> "We've never talked about it much, have we? About love itself, I mean."
>
> He smiled a little. "We never had to."
>
> "I'd sort of like to—now," she said. "Do you mind? I'd like to try to tell you how I feel, before tomorrow—happens...."
>
> "All right," he said. "Tell me about love."
>
> She watched a cloud ravel itself against the moon.

"Well," she said, "to me it's a shining thing, like a golden fire or a silver mist. It comes very quietly; you can't command it, but you can't deny it, either. When it does come, you can't quite see it or touch it, but you can feel it—inside of you and around you and the person you love. It changes you; it changes everything...."

She leaned back, clasping her hands around her knees, the moonlight bright and ecstatic on her face.

"Oh, it's so many little things!...It's holding hands in a movie; it's humming a sad little tune; it's walking in the rain; it's riding in a convertible with the wind in your hair...."

She broke off suddenly and gave him a desolate look...."Maybe I'm just being silly," she said doubtfully. "Is that the way love seems to you?"

He did not answer for a while. At last he said, "I might add a little to your definition."

"You mean, you wouldn't change it?"

"No. Just add to it."

She put her chin in her hands. "Go ahead. I'm listening."

He took out the pipe she had given him and rubbed the smooth grain along his cheek. "You said it was a lot of little things. You're right. I could mention a few that don't have much glitter. But they have an importance that grows....

"Coming home to somebody when day is ended—or waiting for somebody to come home to you. Giving, or getting, a word of praise when none is really deserved. Sharing a joke that nobody else under-stands. Planting a tree together and watching it grow. Sitting up with a sick child. Remembering anniver-saries...

"It's not all triumphant, you know. It's also sharing disappointment and sorrow. It's going out to slay the dragon, and finding the dragon too much for you, and running away—but going out again the next day....It's the gradual acceptance of limitations—your own as well as others'. It's discarding some of the ambitions you had for yourself, and planting them in your children..." His voice trailed off into the listening night.

"Are you talking," she asked finally, "about living, or loving?"

"You'll find there's not much of one without the other."

"When—when did you learn that?"

"Quite a while ago. Before your mother died." His hands touched her shining hair. "Better go to bed now, baby. Tomorrow's your big day."

She clung to him suddenly. "Oh, Daddy, I'm going to miss you so!"

"Nonsense," he said. "I'll be seeing you all the time. Run along now."

But after she was gone, he sat there for a long time, alone in the moonlight.[2]

What a conversation. The daughter will remember a won-derful discussion about love and life with a man who has given her both. The father will remember a lifetime of love—the stories of their life together—that overflowed his heart on the night before his daughter married. Even crisis times have become part of his definition of love, and now he sits alone in the moonlight celebrating his collection of memories.

This book is fundamentally dedicated to turning our limited number of moments with our children into lasting memories. One of our missions, as parents, is to become so aware of the things our kids remember that we are not only present and involved in those events, but we are serving as teachers and guides through them. It would be a great tragedy to spend eighteen years with our children and look back to discover that we are not significantly attached to many of their positive memories.

THE POWER OF STORIES

Our memories are primarily tied to the "stories" of our lives—those events that were laden with emotions, because it's the emotions that make the event memorable. The more intense the emotion, the more vivid the memory. Facts will never motivate response, or even be remembered, like stories will. Actually, stories not only help us remember the facts found within a story, but stories also embed values into events and emotions into images.

That's why stories from children—children of all ages—are interwoven throughout every chapter of this book. Many of them are from children I have talked with for hours. Some are childhood stories collected from adults. Some are stories gleaned from other writers, and some are part of my own collection. Some of the stories have never been told before, many I have told in seminars across America, and others have been told to me after those same seminars. Stories seem to attract other stories. In fact, the stories in this book will probably surface stories in your own life, and chapter nine will explore that phenomenon. When necessary, the names and locations in the stories have been changed to preserve anonymity, and every attempt has been made to give appropriate and accurate credit for each story included in this book.

In these pages everyday people get to speak, and their stories will touch your heart. Over the last three years, through the process of interviewing scores of parents and children, surveying thousands of others, and enjoying hundreds of hours of conversations with parents and kids, I have let them "write" the book. People like you and me, not social scientists or parenting experts, give this book their authenticity and practicality. By sharing from their experience the things kids never forget, real people speak with power about...

> the people who really care,
> the stories that have impacted them,
> the failures they have experienced,
> the milestones of growing up,
> the rules,
> the crisis times,
> and the traditions of home.

At the conclusion of each chapter are Parenting Points—the "what can I do about this?" insight. They give parents practical suggestions for making an impact on the memories of their children. These suggestions are designed to help us make more intentional, positive memories and fewer accidental, negative ones.

The "principles" sprinkled throughout provide an outline of the key points in each chapter. The ones you find most helpful will probably come from the stories you identify with emotionally. That's the way it should be. And, it's okay to write your own moral to a story that touches you.

MAKE THE MOST
OF THE TIME YOU'VE GOT

Whether you live in Junction, Texas, or Los Angeles, California, days seem to be spinning faster and faster. Time does seem to "slip through our fingers like sand."

Perhaps you can identify with Martha. She starts her day wishing her microwave would hurry up. The last time she stopped to smell the roses they were in a can of Glade. And she visits fast food restaurants so frequently that the other day she caught herself ordering into her mailbox and driving around the house.

In this constant state of hurriedness, as parents we may feel not only our time, but our children, slipping through our fingers like sand. Since our time with our youngsters is limited, let's do the things that will be remembered. It is my prayer that as you read *Seven Things Kids Never Forget* your heart and your head will be encouraged to take some action in your life, to reclaim a lost moment, or experience a new one. Don't just read this book. Experience it. Claim the time you have left with your children; otherwise you will identify with Terry.

Terry got off the bus. The shy boy of eight looked up at the poster on the telephone pole. The circus was coming to town. He had never before seen the circus or a circus poster. There were elephants, lions, trapeze artists, and clowns. Uncharacteristically, he tore the poster down and ran home with it clutched in his hand.

He lived with his mother, grandmother, and sister in a small frame house. He showed his mom the circus poster, hoping that somehow he would get to go. With tears in her eyes Terry's mom told him that she was sorry but they didn't have the money for him to go. Terry hugged his mom and cried his way to bed.

Grandma called from the kitchen, "Terry, come here, please." He got up, rubbed the tears from his eyes, and obeyed.

Grandma reached up high on a shelf for an old Mason jar. Terry watched as she poured out the contents on the kitchen table. There was a dollar bill, some quarters, a bunch of dimes, and lots of nickels. It added up to just enough for a matinee admission to the circus.

Terry had never been so excited in his life. Tomorrow was going to be the best! He put the money deep into his pants' pocket and slept in those pants that night.

The next day, after asking, "Is it time yet?" a hundred times, it was time. He ran all the way to town. When he arrived, he saw people of all ages gathered on Main Street. They were talking about how the circus came to town last year, and how great it was, and how everyone loved it. Terry sat down on the curb and listened; he could hardly wait.

Finally someone yelled, "Here it comes!" As the circus paraded down the street, Terry stood there and watched the elephants, trunk to tail, trunk to tail. Next came the lions roaring in their cages. Then the trapeze artists and the acrobats dressed in bright costumes walked right by him. There were clowns everywhere, running back and forth. The last clown was riding a unicycle and throwing candy to all the kids. As the clown passed by, Terry ran up to him, handed him his money, and ran home.

Terry thought he'd been to the circus, but all he had seen was the parade.

It's fun to watch from the curb, but memory making requires more than presence; it requires participation. The joy of parenting is enhanced to the degree we are willing to get involved. Joy is found when we step off the curb and into the circus.

Chapter Two

KIDS NEVER FORGET PEOPLE WHO CARE

Our children are experiencing a firsthand unraveling of the family. The people who are supposed to care the most are disappearing.

Every day more than three children die of injuries inflicted by abusive parents. Nearly ninety kids a day are taken from their parents' custody and added to the overburdened foster care system.

Of the sixty-five million Americans under eighteen years of age, 22 percent live in single parent homes and almost 3 percent live with no parent at all. Back in 1960, the ratio of children living in single parent homes was only one in ten.

Even those numbers underestimate children's experiences because they only give the percentages at a particular time. The federal government estimates that about 61 percent of the children born in 1987 will spend some time in a single parent household before they are eighteen years old. That's nearly two out of every three children.[1]

Set against these statistics on the unraveling of the family, this chapter proclaims a message of hope in an atmosphere of despair. It describes a number of caring moments between parents and children—moments that children remembered into adulthood. In many cases the parents probably have long since forgotten or discounted these caring events. They may have never even realized their children were experiencing an extraordinary moment when some routine event or everyday conversation was deposited into their bank of unforgettable memories.

We begin here because nothing will make a greater difference in a child's life than knowing he has the unconditional love of his parents. Every parent has his own style of demonstrating love; there is no mold for all of us to fit into. But there are principles that undergird these caring moments, whatever our unique style of expressing love may be. And by being more aware of the principles, we can make conscious choices to create more positive memories with our children.

Our limits of time and energy will force us to make choices—tough choices. Caring parents will learn how to make the choices that will have the greatest impact on their children.

MOM'S INFLUENCE

Mom continues to be on the top of everyone's list of caregivers. Robert Munsch and Sheila McGraw teamed up in 1986 to write and illustrate a popular children's book, entitled *Love You Forever*, about the enduring nature and the recyclable power of a mother's love. In it a young mother holds her newborn son and sings,

"I'll love you forever,
I'll like you for always,

As long as I'm living
my baby you'll be."

Sometimes she feels like her boy is driving her crazy, but she still sings.

Sometimes she wants to sell him to the zoo, but she still sings.

Sometimes she feels like she's living in a zoo, but she still sings.

When the boy is grown and gone, and she is old and sick, she can't finish the song, but her boy can. He sings to her,

"I'll love you forever,
I'll like you for always,
As long as I'm living
my Mommy you'll be."[2]

This mother's life of self-denial and self-sacrifice is a powerful demonstration of her caring—so powerful, in fact, that her son knows exactly how to demonstrate his love for her. He does what she has done for him.

Motherhood is, by definition, full-time caring. The question is, after tons of laundry, thousands of fast food orders, endless trips to soccer practice, questionable music lessons, and dozens of uneventful daily routines, does anything stand out enough to be remembered? Here are four mothers who stood out above the mundane and routine—mothers who will never be forgotten.

Marta's Mom Took Action

In *Family Tales, Family Wisdom* author Robert Akeret asks a grandmother named Marta about an interesting old photo of young Marta and her dog. The poor dog looked as if he had been converted into a "doggy ricksha." His hind legs were strapped into a wagonlike contraption, leaving his front legs free to pull him wherever he wanted to go. Marta responded, "That's my dog, Petey....You see, one day he chased a pigeon off our back porch, he thought he could fly, and he landed on the concrete three floors below. Petey lost the use of his back legs, and the vet wanted to put him to sleep, but my mother said no, it would kill me. She had this idea she'd make him this thing with wheels on it, a sling chariot, and she did, and it worked too. He could run and he even got into dogfights."[3]

PRINCIPLE

*Caring moms sometimes do unusual
or even outlandish things
for the benefit of their children.*

Allyson's Mom Was Persistent

Allyson lived with her mom and dad in a small town about twenty miles from Lubbock, Texas. They were a close-knit threesome. To Allyson's fourteen-year-old way of thinking, everything about life was pretty normal.

One Wednesday after school Allyson's mom asked her to go with her to the mall in Lubbock. Allyson agreed, but she wanted to bring a friend. Mom refused, and Allyson got in the car a little miffed, determined to ride to the mall without talking. Mom had a different idea.

Once they turned left onto the main road to Lubbock, Mom announced that it was time to talk about sex. Allyson was shocked; her mother had said the "s" word. Allyson had talked with her friends about sex, she had read about it in magazines, she had learned a little about it in movies and on TV, but she had never imagined talking to her mother about it.

Allyson's mom talked about when she was a young girl. She talked about the world of feelings, affection, love, boys, dating, what was appropriate, and why it was important to talk and set some rules.

Allyson pretended not to listen. She used standard defensive words like, "Mom!" "I can't believe this!" "I know this stuff." "Mom, that's okay, really!" She even tried to slip down in the front seat so that no one would know she was having a conversation with her mother about sex. (Allyson was convinced that every car they passed knew her mother was talking about sex.) The truth is, she listened to and remembered every word.

Five years later Allyson told me about these conversations with her mother. Allyson added, "Those short trips to the mall were the best. Before long we could talk about anything, and we did. I didn't know how rare that experience was until my friends told me how lucky I was; their moms never talked to them."

Allyson's mother persisted in discussing sex with her daughter to prepare her for the future choices she would have to make when Mom wouldn't be around. Caring mothers do that. Allyson needed time and guidance in accepting and understanding the confusing feelings and decisions of adolescence. Caring mothers, like Allyson's, are persistent in providing these moments of preparation.

P R I N C I P L E

Caring moms make time to discuss difficult and critical issues, even if children seem disinterested.

A Mom and Her Presence

One struggling young mother raised six children in the background of the worst poverty-stricken area of Oklahoma City. The children had few possessions. They were poor, fatherless, and often hungry, but they had a resourceful mother with an undaunted spirit. In the middle of the depression, she somehow managed to buy two season tickets to the symphony every year. She took one child with her to each performance, passing down the turns just as she did their clothes.

Even though they all lived in a one-room shack with a dirt floor, they regularly put on their best clothes and hand in hand attended museums, theaters, and the symphony. Their mother couldn't give them many presents, but she could give them a passion for the arts. This courageous young woman helped her children see past the poverty. By sharing moments in the museums and symphonies, she taught them to care about something beyond themselves. She gave them hope.

Although she has been dead for years, her children still benefit from her legacy. Each child is exceptionally creative. One is a successful artist. Another is an architect. Another is a writer. They feel her presence in every art museum, theater, and symphony they visit, and, most importantly, in the way they see themselves.

P R I N C I P L E

Caring moms take their children places where they will be challenged to see beyond themselves. They help children to dream.

Cagney's Mom Held Him Accountable

One of the most significant findings gleaned from the studies of successful kids raised in disastrous families is the difference one caring, inspirational person can make in an otherwise hopeless situation. James Cagney's mom was such a person.

Cagney was born and raised in desperate conditions. He was one of seven children. His father was an alcoholic. Early in life Cagney began working at odd jobs, and by age fourteen he had a regular job. He and his brothers brought every cent home so the family would have enough to eat.

A number of his school friends and street companions wound up in the penitentiary; one died in the electric chair. But Cagney was held accountable by an inspirational person. "We had a mother to answer to," he said. "We loved her profoundly, and our driving force was to do what she wanted because we knew how much it meant to her."[4] Cagney's mother inspired her children to put the needs of the family before their individual needs. She instilled in her children a sense of responsibility, regardless of circumstances. Parents who care hold their children accountable; they inspire morality in the midst of immorality.

P R I N C I P L E

Caring moms expect their children to behave,
and they hold them accountable
for their behavior.

DAD'S INFLUENCE

Country star George Strait sings a wonderful ballad called "Love without End, Amen," which is a story-song about the secret of father-son love.

The first verse tells about a little boy who is caught fighting at school and is sent home. "Fighting was against the rules and it didn't matter why." He practices how best to break the news, and when the dad arrives, the little boy tells him his story, expecting the worst.

But his dad responds, "Let me tell you a secret about a father's love, a secret my daddy said was just between us. He said daddies don't just love their children ever now and then; it's a love without end, amen."[5]

This "love without end" is the promise to love without condition, whether our children become presidents or prisoners. It's not based on what they do or what they become; it's not given as a reward for good behavior or academic achievement. In fact, many times it's given in spite of behavior.

I believe a "new breed" of fathers is arising in our land—ones who place a high priority on being caring fathers, ones who demonstrate their "love without end" by being involved, affectionate, and nurturing. They are taking their role seriously. It reminds me of Malachi 4:5-6, where the prophet tells of a time when the hearts of fathers will turn to their children and the hearts of children to their fathers.

From the Ground Up

Every moment a dad spends playing on the floor with his child is an investment in his child's future, especially in his emotional development. Perhaps Larry's father knew this instinctively.

Larry, a young father from Hobbs, New Mexico, told me about his vivid memories of playtimes with his dad.

At the least expected moment he would pounce on me like a tiger, and the tickle fight was on. He would attack me and then pretend to be dead. Then I would attack him and try to tweak his ribs, but I never could.

He would say, "Okay, we can play Monopoly, or we can read a book, or we can wrestle." I almost always picked wrestling. I would end up being swung around and around until he was too tired to stand. He would rub his whiskers on my face. I would dive on his stomach and roll all around the floor. After a while, he would get down on all fours and I would ride him like a horse. Several times I nearly choked him to death, trying to hold on.

If Mom wasn't home, we would throw pillows at each other. I remember once when he threw a pillow and broke a lamp. We spent the next hour repairing it. It was our secret; I don't think Mom ever found out.

The laughter of those moments on the floor helped me survive the uncertain teenage times when I felt confused and detached.

Although pillow throwing has yet to be confirmed as a significant father-child activity, playtime is the primary way a father communicates his love to a young child. The touching, talking, tickling dad develops trust and security in his children, both girls and boys.

P R I N C I P L E

Caring fathers demonstrate their love
for their young children (boys and girls)
by having fun with them,
by playing with them regularly.

Imperfect Times

My dad was not perfect by any means. He didn't get to spend much time with me as a child—he was either working, sleeping, or drinking most of the time. But I will never forget our deep-sea fishing trip. The older I get, the more I treasure that day as a perfect day with an imperfect man.

I had never been fishing from a boat before, and this boat wasn't on some little lake. It was out in the Pacific Ocean near Half Moon Bay, California. After riding waves up and down for what seemed like hours, we dropped anchor and began baiting hooks. As I stared at the pail of fresh baby squid, I flashed back to scenes of the giant squid in *Twenty Thousand Leagues under the Sea*.

Seeing my expression, the captain laughed, "They won't hurt you, but their mommy might."

Embarrassed and a little peeved, I picked up one of those ugly creatures, stuck it on my hook, and just as I was about to cast the greatest cast in the world, my dad grabbed the pole. "Whoa," he said. "Out here there's no need to cast. We're already in the deep water."

With great disappointment I let the line drop over the edge of the boat. Truth was, I had never been fishing when you actually caught fish, but I really loved to cast.

In less than a minute it felt like a whale had latched on to my hook. I struggled just to hold on to the pole.

"I think you've got a big one," Dad said. "Just keep the line tight, and you'll wear him out."

My mind was filled with images of a fish too big for the boat. I was having the time of my life. My dad stopped fishing and just watched me.

The fish turned out to weigh a mere eight pounds, but before the day was over, I caught fifteen more about that same size, and I became an expert in undoing backlashes on my reel.

Dad and I talked about going deep-sea fishing again, but we never did. That one trip had to last a lifetime. I now regret that I never told him how important that day was to me. As I grow older, my memory of that one day overshadows the memories of times he wasn't there.

PRINCIPLE

Caring dads don't have to be perfect, but they have to spend one-on-one time with their children.

Surprise Times

Chuck Swindoll tells an unforgettable story of a father from Montgomery, Alabama, who had a flair for surprises. He and his family had planned a summer camping trip along California's coastal Highway 1. They had been looking forward to the trip for months, but now there would have to be a change of plans.

Dad announced that some unexpected problems had come up at work and he would have to stay home. But he wanted them to go on without him. He would be with them in spirit. He knew where they would be at any given time; he even knew within the hour when they would cross the Great Divide.

Reluctantly they packed all the camping equipment into the station wagon and headed off on their great adventure, minus Dad. Once they were out , he put his surprise into action.

He had arranged to fly to an airport near where his family would be on a particular day. When he arrived, he had a friend pick him up and drive him to a spot on the interstate by which his family would have to pass. Then he sat just off the road on his sleeping bag and waited to see the familiar station wagon.

Before long he spotted the car packed full of camping equipment, eager kids, and his wife. He stepped out onto the shoulder of the road and stuck out his thumb.

"Mom," the youngster riding shotgun yelled, "that guy looks like...DAD!"[6]

What a memory for those children! Surprises make the greatest impact in the shortest period of time. And you can bet this father made an impact on his children. Not all of us can go to such extravagant lengths to plan a surprise, but all of us can at times make an effort to surprise our families in delightful ways. It can be as simple as mailing a card to your children, or calling during the day to talk to them, or waking them up in the middle of a winter night to play in the freshly fallen snow, as I did once with my family. The point is that the father creates an out-of-the-ordinary experience to delight his family.

P R I N C I P L E

*Caring fathers find ways to surprise and
delight their families.*

GRANDPARENT INFLUENCE

As parents we will never be able to do all the nurturing, all the caring, ourselves. We weren't meant to. Grandparents were meant to help, because they can do things that parents can't. In a special and unique way, they can provide balance, understanding, perspective, and acceptance.

Autumn (age 7) explained, "The only people who have time to really listen or to read the whole story without skipping pages are grandparents."

"They call on the phone and want to talk to me and my dog," volunteered Paul (age 5).

Gary (age 9) said, "My granny tells me secrets about my parents."

"They can tell you what you ought to do without giving you a lecture," Liz (age 10) reported.

"They're the only adults with time," Jenny (age 11) concluded.

Grandparents Lend Perspective

Grandparents help parents relax and stay on the planet. And children can benefit greatly from a wholesome set of caring grandparents who lend a broader perspective, as Missy discovered.

"I could never be like my mom. She's always so cool. She never gets excited and says dumb things like I do," Missy moaned.

"Did I ever tell you about the first time your mother decided to cook breakfast?" Grandma laughed. "She caught all the bacon grease in the frying pan on fire. So she grabbed the pan, still flaming, and ran out of the house down to the corner fire station yelling at the top of her voice, 'Fire! Fire!' She had the firemen put it out and then noticed that she was wearing only her shorty pajamas. She called us from the fire station, and your grandfather had to drive down one block, take her bathrobe, and then drive her back home. She wouldn't walk down the street for a month after that."[7]

But not all problems are so easily solved. Grandparents with their experience and informed perspective can bring wisdom and insight to a situation that appears hopeless to the child. Roger was fortunate in having just such a grandparent.

It was in the sixties, and my parents were continually on my back about my long hair. It was a really big deal with them. One day things just got out of hand. I was in my room with the headphones on listening to the Beatles. They barged in, tied me up with rope, sat on top of me, and with scissors in hand they cut my shoulder length hair to the bobbed length they wanted.

I was livid. They walked out of the room, leaving me tied up with a mess to clean. I lay there fuming and scheming ways to get even. I don't know how long it was before my grandpa came by, but I remember what he did. He looked at me lying there on the floor, untied the ropes, handed me a New York Yankee's ball cap to wear, and took me for a drive in his old pickup.

We didn't talk much on the way to the beach. Once there, he bought me a hot dog, and we started walking. Grandpa talked about when he was a kid, about when my father was a kid, and about my life as a kid. And we talked about what it takes to grow up when life seems unfair.

Finally, Grandpa stopped and pointed out toward the horizon. "You see this ocean," he said. "It's always here for you. Whether your hair is long or short, it's here for you." Somehow that ocean and those words softened my anger. That old man gave me more than an ocean that day; he gave me a piece of himself.

His intervention helped me face the days ahead. Years later, after my grandpa died, when I was going through a personal crisis, I found myself at that same beach. As I walked up and down the sand, I could hear those wise words again, and I knew I could face whatever lay ahead.[8]

Grandparents who care serve as a bridge between parent and child when needed. They can help each side step back from the edge and get back in balance. Parents who refuse to give the grandparents this opportunity for involvement are missing a great support resource.

P R I N C I P L E

Caring parents provide time for grandparents
and grandchildren to share the secrets
and perspectives of their worlds.
Grandparents can be a valued resource
not only for the kids but also for the parents.

Raymond's Story

After attending a family retreat in Kansas City, I received a letter from Raymond. During the weekend he had remembered an incident from when he was eight years old that had made a strong impression.

Grandma and I were Christmas shopping in the mall and having a wonderful time. Everyone seemed to be in such a rush, but not Grandma. She never seemed to be in a hurry when we shopped; in fact we made a game of it.

While we were drinking one of those strawberry fruit drinks at the food court, the first grader sitting at the table next to us was having a terrible time. He was whining, crying, throwing fits, and yelling no at the top of his lungs. He was making everyone around him miserable.

Finally, my grandma took a notepad out of her purse, leaned over to where the little boy was sitting, got his attention, and asked, "Could you tell me your name?"

He stopped whining for a moment, looked at her and her notepad, and said, "Matt."

Grandma wrote down *Matt*.

"Who are you?" the boy asked.

"I work for Santa Claus," Grandma said, "and I'm taking the names of children who are being mean and ugly. Now, what's your last name?"

"No, I'll be good. I promise," he quickly responded.

His mother thanked my grandma, and we continued our shopping. We never talked about that little boy, and I was never quite sure that my grandma was kidding about working for Santa, so I was especially good around her.

Humor is disarming and stress reducing. We need daily doses. Grandparents can be wonderful sources of laughs, and playfulness, and occasionally even surprising adventures.

P R I N C I P L E

Caring parents encourage grandparents to share
their strengths with the grandchildren.
If it's humor and playfulness,
then everyone will be blessed.

UNFORGETTABLE CHARACTERS

Unforgettable characters like favorite uncles or aunts, eccentric neighbors, teachers, and friends help children test and expand their view of life. Children from single parent families use these people to piece together their image of the missing parent. These people encourage temporary excursions into the world outside the security of home. Each excursion stirs emotions, changes our view of others, and sharpens our focus on life. Caring parents will see these excursions as friends, not enemies, because these colorful relationships help shape the character of our children.

My Uncle Said Yes

In the summer before my third grade year, I was invited to spend a week on Angel Island, just off Tiburon in the San Francisco Bay. My uncle Cliff, a state park ranger for California, had been assigned for the summer months to the deserted, yet-to-be-opened park on the island, and he asked me to come along. It was a dream come true for any eight-year-old boy. It was, in fact, the best seven-day adventure of my childhood.

The only transportation on the island was an old, red fire truck. At least once a day we rode around the island, running the siren just for fun. During the week we caught crabs, fished off the pier, biked all over the island, ate dinner at the lighthouse, and stayed up late telling stories and listening to the foghorn.

As I look back, all the days were full of adventure, but the first day was outstanding. We were loading supplies on the boat that would take us over to the island when one of Cliff's buddies offered to take Cliff Jr. and me across via helicopter. I couldn't believe it when Cliff said yes. It seemed that my parents always said no to fun things. If the first thing out of their mouth wasn't no, it was, "Don't even ask."

After the boat took off, the pilot strapped us in and up we went. It was so noisy we couldn't talk, but we could see everywhere. We flew low around the shoreline and landed just before the boat arrived. None of my friends had ever ridden in a helicopter, and I couldn't wait to tell them all about it. I still couldn't believe Cliff had said yes. That summer, at that very moment, he became my favorite uncle.

P R I N C I P L E

Caring parents are willing to let their children spend time with people who can expand their horizons in positive ways.

A Teacher Changed Lives

For many children a schoolteacher, or coach, or a Sunday School teacher makes an impact that lasts a lifetime. Parents who care will build a team relationship with these special people that will help tie the child's home world and school world together. Many of the most important tests our children will take are not academic; they are social, moral, and spiritual. And, in one way or another, all children will face these tests at school; therefore, it is critical that parents and teachers not only be communicating with each other but also be in harmony in their goals for the children. Then the teachers' impact on our children will augment and enhance the foundation that we as parents have built.

Probably all of us remember some teachers particularly well, perhaps for their enthusiasm or giftedness, their idiosyncrasies or their pet peeves, but Mark's teacher will be remembered for the best reason of all—she cared about her students.

Mark was a student at St. Mary's School in St. Paul, Minnesota. He was one of those students you couldn't help but love, but this story is not really about Mark.

One Friday everything seemed to be going wrong. The students had worked all week on a new concept of math, and they were frustrated and discouraged. The teacher decided she had to stop the crankiness before it got out of hand, so she suggested a break. She asked them to list the names of the students in the class and to leave a space after each name. Then she told them to think of the nicest things they could say about each of their classmates and write it down. It took the remainder of the class period.

That Saturday the teacher wrote down the name of each student on a separate piece of paper, and then she listed what everyone had said about that individual. On Monday she gave each student his or her list.

No one ever mentioned those papers in class again. The group of students moved on, and so did the teacher.

Years passed. Then one night after returning home from a long trip, the teacher learned that Mark had been killed in Vietnam. The funeral was the next day, and his parents wanted her to attend.

One by one, those who loved Mark walked by the coffin. His teacher was one of the last to pass by. As she did, a pall-bearer asked if she was Mark's math teacher. She nodded.

"Mark talked a lot about you," the soldier said.

After the funeral, most of Mark's former classmates gathered at his house. "We want to show you something," Mark's mother whispered to the teacher. "They found this paper inside Mark's wallet." The old notebook paper had been taped and folded and retaped many times. It was that old list they had made in math class. Mark's mother continued, "Thank you for doing that. As you can see, he treasured it."

Mark's classmates gathered around. Charlie smiled sheepishly and said, "I still have my list in the top drawer of my desk at home." Chuck's wife said that he had asked her to put his in their wedding album. "And I have mine, too," Marilyn said. "It's in my diary."

Vickie reached into her purse and pulled out her wallet and showed her torn list from the class. "I think we all kept them."[9]

Mark's teacher was remembered because she was interested in more than math skills. She showed her students that she cared about them as people, and she helped them see the good in themselves and others. Consequently, she will be forever connected to those students and the intense feelings experienced that day.

PRINCIPLE

Caring parents will build a team relationship with those people who are significantly involved in the lives of their children.

WHERE DO WE BEGIN?

Perhaps where Jenny, in the wisdom of her ten years, began.

The mall seemed to be unusually crowded, and their excursion had run long, but as Jenny and her mom walked past the Hallmark Shop, Jenny stopped. She begged her mom for just one more minute. She had almost forgotten to buy a birthday card for her favorite teacher.

Mom gave permission and sat down on a nearby bench for the short wait. She waited and waited and waited.

Just as Mom was about to march into the store and retrieve her thoughtless child, Jenny emerged with her arm around Katie Beth, one of her neighborhood friends.

With one quick glance Jenny saw the glare in Mom's eyes. Jenny had become so involved with Katie Beth that she had forgotten all about the card.

"Just what have been doing, young lady?" snapped Mom. "Where is your card?"

"Mom, Katie Beth was really sad because she misses her dad. He has been gone for weeks. She was looking for just the right card to send him. She was crying, and I tried to help," explained Jenny.

"So, did you help her find a card?" Mom questioned.

"No," Jenny replied, "I helped her cry."

Some of the best lessons on parenting are learned from our children. The first step in caring for anyone is identifying with that person's situation. Caring parents start by coming to understand the feelings of their child. The Bible makes a lot of practical sense when it says, "Rejoice with those who rejoice, and weep with those who weep."[10]

For Mom

In relationship to God: Pray that God will give you the energy to make the most of the time you've got with your kids.

In relationship to your children: Share your passion with your kids. Whether you love art, cooking, baseball, gardening, sewing, jogging, or some other activity, give each of your children the opportunity to join you in your activity. Help them to share a little in your passion (even if they think it's crazy). They may not develop the same intensity of interest as you have, but they will learn something about you and the importance of caring for something beyond themselves.

For Dad

In relationship to God: Ask God to help you keep your time with your kids on the top of your priority list.

In relationship to your children: Surprise your family with a new game. Learn the rules ahead of time (yes, you may have to read the instructions), and get everyone to play. Call it your Family Game Night. The game could be a board game, an outdoors game, or a game you played when you were a child. Remember, the important thing is not who wins; it's having fun. End the time with hugs and an ice cream cone.

For the Parent-Grandparent Connection

In relationship to God: Pray that the Lord will help you know how to involve your parents in the lives of your kids without getting into conflicts over how to raise them. Pray that he will help you learn to work together.

In relationship to your children: Get everybody (parents, kids, grandparents) together for an evening. Set up an audio tape recorder or a video camera to record your activity without interruption. The discussion question for the evening is "What funny things happened to you when you were a kid?" Be prepared to start the discussion by telling a funny thing that happened to you. Encourage everyone to share at least one memory.

For the Parent-Other Person Connection

In relationship to God: Pray that God will give you insight into the strengths of the people who share your children's life with you.

In relationship to your children: Get to know all the adults who spend time with your children. Put their names on your prayer list. Then, as you work with these people, determine to look for strengths in their character and personality. Encourage your child to see the strengths in them. Write a note to each person, thanking him or her for the time and influence with your child.

STEP ONE

In relationship to God: Ask God to help you be more effective in sharing feelings with your children. Ask him to help you do the caring, and let him do the curing.

In relationship to your children: Work with your children on a service project, any kind that helps other people. Take pictures during the project. Then use the pictures to review the time. Ask "what" questions like "What was happening here?" and "What were the people feeling?" The goal is to focus on a shared experience of caring for other people.

Chapter Three

KIDS NEVER FORGET THE STORIES THEY HEAR

When I asked several college students to recall stories they heard as they were growing up, I discovered the importance of having a regular story time. The young adults who had read and been read to regularly had memories full of stories.

Leslie said, "For us, bedtime was story time. We would cuddle up in our beds, and Dad would read one of our favorites, or sometimes he would make up a story or tell an adventure story from his childhood. We still have those storybooks he read to us."

Lori related, "When we would go on short trips or vacations, our time in the car was filled with stories. Mom was best at reading them because she used character voices and got real dramatic. Sometimes we would beg to go on a trip just to hear more stories."

"Birthdays were special story times for me," Jon chimed in. "My parents would join together in telling the story of my life.

They used pictures and things they had saved from my childhood to keep the story moving along. After a while, I knew their story about me was better than my own. I loved it."

"I don't remember a time as much as a place," recalled Reed. "When we built a fire in the fireplace, it seemed as if we always got around to telling stories. My dad would start it and would tell the same old stories, and we enjoyed it every time. I think there was something hypnotic about the flames."

"I remember going camping a lot when I was a kid. As soon as it got dark, we gathered around the campfire, and someone would start with 'Remember when...' and the stories would run for hours. I really miss those times," PJ said.

Beno added, "We had a story time candle. Every time Mom told us stories, one of us got to light the candle. I loved to watch it burn as my mom read the stories. Those were some of the best times of my childhood."

Robert Coles, Pulitzer Prize winning author of numerous books on childhood, has spent more time listening to children than anyone else in the last twenty-five years. He suggests that children are profoundly influenced in their decisions by the stories they have heard. For instance, children who have grown up without hearing and reading stories have a difficult time dealing with suffering. Generally people can handle suffering if it has some purpose, but if there is no purpose, the goal is never to suffer. Shared stories give children a perspective beyond their own, a chance to see how someone else faced difficulties and overcame them and even grew because of them. Vicariously children are taken from suffering to solutions. Through the characters in the stories, children begin to see how beliefs and values affect people's lives, and children begin to incorporate them into their own lives.

Stories—family stories, read-aloud stories, original stories, and

Bible stories—have great value within a family. They provide opportunities to be together, to talk, to ask questions, to learn about each other, to explore the world beyond the family circle, to discuss values and decisions, life and death. They stir the imagination, touch the heart, and create entire worlds out of precious moments. The power of storytelling with the family could hardly be overestimated.

RETELLING FAMILY STORIES

Following the television presentation of Alex Haley's *Roots*, there was a nationwide explosion in researching family genealogies. Since that time, it seems there is at least one person in every extended family who makes a hobby of tracing the family tree. But family history is more than filling in names on a chart. Family history is the story of courtships and feuds, heroes and mischief-makers. Family stories help children find their place in the family, and they give children a solid sense of connection and belonging. And that linkage to others wards off the feelings of isolation and lack of accountability to others that can be so detrimental.

I took the opportunity recently to visit my aunt Ruby and to explore a bit of my family's history. It had been thirty-four years since I had seen her. She now seemed a foot shorter and more weathered by age, but she was still full of spunk. I was curious about her view of life, so I asked her, "Ruby, what's the most exciting thing to happen to you in the last thirty years?"

She put her tea glass down on her TV tray, and while getting up she said, "Well, come in here and I'll show you."

I got up and followed her to the kitchen where she beamed with pride as she pointed to the corner. "There it is," she boasted. "My Maytag. It's the best thing I can remember."

While we were up, she showed me through the house. There was a console TV in every room, including the bathroom. In the breakfast area of the kitchen a large console model almost filled the room. Sitting on top of the console was a tabletop model, and on top of it was a little portable. I didn't even ask.

But Ruby volunteered, "Well, the bottom one doesn't work, but it's so pretty I just wanted to keep it. The middle one's picture works, but the sound doesn't. And the little one's sound works, but the picture doesn't."

"Makes sense," I said.

As we returned to the living room, I asked her about one of our more unbelievable family stories—the time her house was picked up by a tornado and then blown apart, scattering family members across the countryside.

Ruby popped up her Lazy-Boy recliner and eagerly began. "First it was a cyclone. This was Arkansas; Texas has tornadoes. Anyway, the storm lifted our wood-framed house right off the ground. The kids were screamin' and hollerin', but the roar of the storm was so loud you could barely hear 'em. We were all inside, rolling around the floor, trying to find something to hold on to. Finally, Durwood decided he wanted to see what was happening outside. Since the windows were boarded up, he crawled over to the door, and when he opened it, the house blew apart. Our eight kids were scattered all over the county, but no one was hurt bad. However, we were still finding clothes and stuff from the house years after that."

My dad liked to tell about walking two miles to school, uphill both ways. And he had to do a full day's work on the farm every day before he left for school. My mom took turnip and onion sandwiches for lunch. And they both stuffed newspapers inside their shoes during the winter to keep their feet warm.

When I was young, I complained about these stories, but now I treasure them. And now I pass on to my daughters not only my parents' stories but also my own stories—stories about the night our house slid down the hill, the day my brother and sister set fire to the house, my first "crush," and the day Tim was killed and I was thrown out of the car to safety. They are part of my legacy.

Although these stories may get mixed with a little fantasy through the years, they serve an important purpose. They relate the experiences—people, places, and events—that are part of our history. They relate our perspective—our beliefs, feelings, and attitudes. And they relate our insight—the new awareness gained by the experience. Whether we realize it or not, our stories are remembered for a reason. Maybe it was our newfound courage, or persistence, or perhaps the way our problem was solved.

<u>P R I N C I P L E</u>

Family stories are a gift to our children,
a gift of connection and insight,
a gift that will be appreciated more as they grow older.
Children need to hear the stories even before they can
appreciate what they are gaining from them.

But family stories shouldn't be limited to tales of parents and grandparents, eccentric cousins, and renegade aunts and uncles. Like Jon, whose parents retold his story every birthday, every child enjoys hearing the stories of what he has contributed to the family's life—the fun, the successes, the near catastrophes. A child never tires of hearing his story, and through it he is reminded of his value and place in the family.

Leslie will likely hear this story retold on her.

At the beginning of the summer Leslie's mother decided it was time to give her fourteen-year-old daughter the responsibility of washing the clothes. She was to make sure they were washed and dried, folded and put away.

For two months Leslie faithfully did her job. One day as her mom was heading to the store, she asked Leslie if she needed any laundry supplies.

"What kind of supplies?" Leslie asked.

"Well, laundry soap for one thing," her mother replied.

"Soap? Are you supposed to use soap?" came the startled answer.

P R I N C I P L E

Family stories come from the kids, too.
The retelling of humorous and positive events
in the children's lives reinforces for them
their unique worth to the family.

If our children learn from us only how to behave in public, how to color coordinate their clothes, and what makes us mad, then they don't really know us. By telling them our stories, we reveal our values, our beliefs, and our growing understanding of life, and even our willingness to laugh at our own mistakes and be human. Family stories help our children get to know the real people they call Mom and Dad.

READING STORIES ALOUD

Although retelling family stories can be an important part of family life at any age, when children are small, there is a window of opportunity for parents to have a great impact on their children by reading to them. Jim Trelease, the Johnny Appleseed of the read-aloud movement, has spent fifteen years planting the thought that one of the most important things parents can do is read to their children. He has authored two popular resource books for parents, *The New Read-Aloud Handbook* and *Hey! Listen to This,* in which he encourages parents to set aside a few minutes for a story every day. The real danger is not that parents will bore their children with stories, but that a child will grow up never being read to at all. In *The New Read-Aloud Handbook* he tells why: "I read because my father read to me. And because he had read to me, when my time came I knew intuitively there is a torch that is supposed to be passed from one generation to the next. And through countless nights of reading I began to realize that when enough of the torchbearers stop passing the torches, a culture begins to die."[1]

Reading aloud to children is one of those rare treats that they like and that's good for them. Children from ages two to ten love good stories, and some of the better stories are enjoyed regardless of a person's age. Children will snuggle close so they can hear every word. They will remember the story and little things about you—the shirt you had on, the warmth of your touch, the sound of your voice. For those moments, time stands still and the story is everything.

In an excellent book entitled *From Wonder to Wisdom* Dr. Charles Smith explains why reading good stories is so important in the parent-child relationship: "Their minds, linked by their imaginations, journey together across the dramatic landscape of the story. Together they witness a tragic loss and heart-breaking grief, a betrayal, a danger confronted, a successful rescue. For twenty minutes, time is suspended. Troubles at school, work, or home recede. While the magic of the moment rules, nothing matters but the story—will the princess ever be happy again?"[2]

During a workshop on the power of storytelling, a participant related a newspaper account of how a story saved a mother's life. The mother and her young son, a grade-schooler, were involved in a car wreck that left her unable to move. The youngster struggled to pull his mother from the car and up an incline away from the wreck. The only thing the mother remembers is the boy's words. As he struggled to pull her away from danger, she heard him saying over and over, "I think I can, I think I can, I think I can!"[3]

Because of *The Little Engine that Could*, so could he.

PRINCIPLE

Read-aloud stories plant seeds of what to do and when to do it, seeds that will grow into character.

TELLING ORIGINAL STORIES

As early as Chase can remember, her father made up stories about her, stories that were full of spunk and adventure. But when she became a parent herself, Chase was overwhelmed by a "bad case of mental confetti." There never seemed to be enough time. Sleep had become a distant memory. Story times were out of the question.

When her daughter was six months old, Chase says, "I was running on empty, tearing through the market, a picture of frazzled competence." One year into parenthood she had become the ultimate worrywart. "But after two years of astounding mutual distractibility," Chase says, "I had a child who could understand basic language—even if she couldn't speak it perfectly herself.

"One night…I told her I had a wonderful surprise for her but she had to be in the crib first. I dimmed the lights, lay down on the welcome bed, reached my hand to hers, and, holding it, told her a story. Flat on my back, I made it up. She listened for a full, motionless five minutes. Yes. Five. The story seemed to come out of thin air. I decided then and there that I would do it again. She had been deeply interested; and I had so enjoyed it."[4]

For more than fifteen years now, Chase Collins has been inventing bedtime stories for her children, as her father did for her. She has shown her children in a fun-filled, caring way that they can face difficulties and grow just like the characters in her stories. She is imparting more than the stories; she is teaching values.

The same is true for you. The values that you hold dear will affect the motives, the solutions, and the rewards in the tales you create.

If you treasure independence and freedom, you will likely find yourself telling stories about astronauts, pioneers, or trapped youngsters.

If you want more kindness in the world, you will invent characters with compassion, wallets with enough money to house the homeless, or a magic potion that can heal hatred.

If you believe in hard work, you will invent tools and machines for your characters. And your story may take place over a long period of time, allowing your hero to solve the mystery or reach the top.

If you value setting goals and then going after them, you may spin yarns about athletes or other characters who face unbelievable odds and still win.

If the prospect of creating a story out of thin air is intimidating, consider the following. At its most basic, every story is about a hero or heroine who must deal with some difficulty and come back a wiser person. You might build your stories from this outline:

Once upon a time...

The hero/heroine had to go on a journey to...

When faced by the unforeseen difficulty of...

The hero/heroine found a way out by...

and returned wiser and stronger because...

And they all lived happily ever after.

The stories we create will connect us, soul to soul, to our children. They will teach the values we hold dear, while providing a setting in which we and our children can share the deepest parts of ourselves. It is important that these stories have a positive resolution—that the characters overcome the difficulties and grow through the experiences—so that the children are always left with hope.

P R I N C I P L E

Creating your own stories for your children connects you emotionally with them and allows you to share the values you hold most dear.

SHARING ETERNAL STORIES

Ted Koppel of ABC's *Nightline* program made one of the most significant commencement speeches of 1987. In addressing the graduates of Duke University, he called for a search for truth in the midst of an overabundance of facts. He made this analysis of our fact-filled society: "In the place of truth, we have discovered facts. For moral absolutes, we have substituted moral ambiguity. We now communicate with everyone and say absolutely nothing. We have reconstructed the Tower of Babel, and it is a television antenna: a thousand voices producing a daily parody of democracy, in which everyone's opinion is afforded equal weight regardless of substance or merit."[5]

Information is power, and we have overdosed on it. Yet while we struggle to acquire more facts, we are at a loss to make sense out of the facts we've got. In the process of acquiring the information, we have forgotten the story—the values and perspective—that ties all the facts together. Only within a context do we discover that some facts are important, some are distractions, and some don't matter at all. The story forces us to interpret and evaluate the facts; it puts all the pieces together so they make sense.

I know scores of concerned parents who subscribe to every parenting magazine they can find. They have parenting facts to the max, but they are still extremely frustrated. Many feel lost and overwhelmed with the task of parenting. In some futile way they believe they will find the answer in some yet-to-be-discovered list of facts. So they continue their struggle to determine what's important and what's not, what's right and what's wrong.

I'm glad the Bible is not a spiritual "Facts on File" book or a book of lists. If it were, we would resort to memorizing facts, testing for facts, and limiting our life to the pursuit of spiritual facts. We would be forever searching for God and never finding him. Our spiritual life would consist of trying to connect the dots without ever seeing the whole picture. God's book is much more than that.

Throughout my life, I have seen the Bible from at least five different viewpoints. One of my earliest memories is of a Sunday School teacher with a big Bible on her lap. She would open that Bible, pull people out of its pages, and magically stick them on the blue board at her side. I remember going home and looking for little people in our big Bible at home, but all it had was dried leaves and flowers, old wedding napkins, and strange papers. At that point in my life, the Bible was a mystery book—special and important, but mysterious.

Then in grade school I discovered the Bible was full of wonderful, exciting stories. Every Saturday night my mother would help me learn my Bible story for Sunday morning, and before long I knew the stories better than many of my Sunday School teachers.

In junior and senior high the Bible became an ethics book, our source of right and wrong. We debated the issues and refined our arguments.

In college I began viewing the Bible as a book of theology—the study of God. By using it like a textbook I could study about God. I learned big religious words like *justification, sanctification, revelation*—all the "ation" words.

Then, after years of ministry, I finally discovered the Bible to be the diary of God, a journal of his involvement with this world and its people. By thinking of the pages as diary entries, I have found it easier to keep my focus on getting to "know" God, not just know about him. When I read the stories of the Bible, I feel as if God is revealing his secrets. In this way, the whole Bible becomes an open invitation to relationship.

P R I N C I P L E

Bible stories help children grow from wondering about God to gaining personal wisdom from God. To learn about him we've got to read his diary. And for young children, hearing the great stories of the Bible is an excellent way to begin learning about God.

When our children are young, it is important to share the Bible's stories any way we can—by reading them, updating them into modern settings, or by acting them out. Here are a few of my favorite stories that are particularly appropriate for children today.

Joseph—a story of character (Genesis 37:12-36; 39:1—50:20). Joseph's trip to Egypt is just the beginning of his testing program. From being imprisoned as a slave to being Pharaoh's right-hand man, Joseph is an excellent example of godly character and forgiveness and turning difficult circumstances into good. I particularly love the famous line, "You meant evil against me, but God meant it for good" (50:20). One lesson that can be taught with this story is that God is with us even when he is silent.

Elijah the caveman (1 Kings 18:16—19:18). Elijah has just come from one of the most dramatic experiences recorded in the Bible—the contest at Mt. Carmel. Then, because of a woman's threat, he runs and hides in a cave on Sinai, God's mountain. When God asks, "Why are you here?" Elijah says that he is the only person left who is true to God and he is in the cave to protect God's investment. This story helps point out the difference between God's perspective and ours, as well as the power of one negative person to spoil our perspective.

Jehoshaphat and the ambush (2 Chronicles 20:1-30). The city is surrounded, and rescue seems out of the question. Out of options, Jehoshaphat calls all the people together and, in essence, gives the problem to God and waits for him to act. All the families just stand there, waiting for God's decision. The next day they win the battle—by singing. One application from this story is to take our problems to God and let him handle them his way and then praise him for the solutions.

Jesus heals the blind man twice (Mark 8:22-26). This little miracle has touched my life a number of times, because I often need that second touch in order to see things more clearly. You can share with your children ways in which we miss seeing the people for the trees. It can also open up discussions about times when God has touched you and helped you see things more clearly.

Peter's surprising release from jail (Acts 12:1-19). Peter is led out of prison by an angel and goes straight to Mary's house where the disciples are praying for his release. But in her excitement over hearing his voice, Rhoda forgets to open the door for him, and those praying inside think she is crazy. This story illustrates the power of prayer and God's surprising answers. Look for surprises.

In a world of shifting morality, Bible stories provide a baseline. Bible stories put the meat on our spiritual bones. Without them, wisdom—understanding how the facts fit together—dies. Sharing Bible stories helps us get close to God, and to each other. What a great picture—two generations reading God's diary and sharing God's secrets.

WHERE DO WE BEGIN?

Start telling stories today. Pick one of these four types of stories, whichever you are most comfortable with: family stories that connect us from generation to generation; read-aloud stories that stimulate imagination, emotions, and interests; original stories that reveal our values and allow our imaginations free rein; or Bible stories that impart the drama of the most important story in the world.

Retelling Family Stories

In relationship to God: Ask God to help you feel more comfortable telling stories about yourself and your family.

In relationship to your children: Schedule a family story night at your house. Invite some friends if you like. Prepare the adults for the storytelling time by asking them to come ready to tell at least one story. Each person can tell about some special event in his childhood, some person or experience that changed his view of the world, some new insight he discovered. Encourage the adults to tell their stories, and then ask if the children have a story they would like to share. They will!

Reading Children's Stories

In relationship to God: Pray that God will help you select and read the stories that are just what your child needs at the moment.

In relationship to your children: Ask a group of parents to come to your house and bring the books that they have used with their children. Meet with several different groups. Then build your own list of quality children's books. The following list could be a beginning spot.

The Man Who Could Call Down Owls, by Eve Bunting—The consequences of selfish abuse of power.

The Nightingale, by Hans Christian Andersen—You don't know what you've got until you lose it.

I'll Always Love You, by Hans Wilhelm—Tell people you love them while you can.

The Changing Maze, by Zilpha Keatley Snyder—A story of risk and a compassionate rescue.

The Boy Who Held Back the Sea, by Lenny Hort—Protecting others in danger.

Sleeping Beauty, retold by Mercer Mayer—Learning to stick to the task, among other themes.

Where the Wild Things Are, by Maurice Sendak—Learning to confront fear.

Albert's Toothache, by Barbara Williams—The frustration of being misunderstood.

Hansel and Gretel, by Jacob and Wilhelm Grimm—Devotion between children.

Little House in the Big Woods, by Laura Ingalls Wilder—This book behind the famous *Little House on the Prairie* TV series is filled with warm stories, family values, and wholesome relationships.

The Unicorn and the Lake, by Marianna Mayer—Using your strength to help others.

The Chronicles of Narnia, by C. S. Lewis—These adventures into imagination are an education in virtue for all ages.

Cheaper by the Dozen, by Frank Gilbreth, Jr. and Ernestine Gilbreth Carey—This fun book describes the adventures of growing up in a family with twelve boisterous children.

Creating Your Own Stories

In relationship to God: Turn your create-a-story time over to God and ask him to help you create the stories that will be best for you and your child.

In relationship to your children: Find an object in the room, such as a stuffed animal, a ball glove, or an old shoe, and make up a story about an adventure that object goes on once the lights are turned off. Follow the outline in this chapter and make sure the hero "lives happily ever after."

Sharing Eternal Stories

In relationship to God: Pray that God will help you pick five Bible stories that you can tell aloud at a moment's notice.

In relationship to your children: Begin a one-on-one time with your child by telling him one of your favorite Bible stories. Don't make this a Bible lesson; just have fun. After you have told five of your favorite stories, ask your child to tell you his or her favorites. You may find you have some favorites in common.

STEP ONE

Ask God for the courage to become a storytelling parent.

1. Pick one of the four kinds of stories discussed in this chapter.

2. Practice. Set a time, and work your storytelling wonder. Don't try to be perfect, and don't let video or audio tapes substitute for you. Nothing and no one can take your place as the storyteller in your children's lives.

3. Start today, wherever you are most comfortable. Just do it.

Chapter Four

KIDS NEVER FORGET FAILURE

E very broken promise, every lost election, and every personal failure has an up side just waiting to be discovered beyond the pain. If we allow ourselves, we will, in fact, learn more from our failures than our successes. We certainly will remember them as much as our successes, and so do our kids. The important thing is *what* we remember from our failures—and what we teach our kids by our response to failure.

WHEN CHILDREN FAIL

One of the most neglected tasks of parenting is the unheralded job of teaching our children how to fail. And failures will come...

> when children have worked countless hours on a campaign for class president and then lose, even though all the kids say they voted for them.

when children have studied hard for the test that would have kept them out of summer school, but fail because they studied the wrong material.

when daughters mess up during cheerleader tryouts and don't make the squad, even though they are better than some of the girls who made it.

when teenagers fail to do what they promised and no excuses will work.

Helping children accept failures and learn from them taxes the skills of even the most veteran parents. But Jeff's dad began at the right spot.

It was going to be a Championship Little League game Jeff would never forget. Virtually the whole town had traveled the fifty miles to watch their youngsters play. Not just parents, mind you, but neighbors, teachers, preachers, and even girls came.

It was a tight game. By the bottom of the ninth Jeff's team was ahead by only one run. After two quick hits, a walk, a run-saving, diving catch by the center fielder, and an infield pop fly, the opposing team's best hitter came to the plate. He swung wildly at the first two pitches, then stepped out of the batter's box, checked with his coach, and stepped back in. The tension mounted as he stood there letting the pitcher take the count to three balls and two strikes.

Then, on the next pitch the batter hit the ball straight to Jeff at shortstop. Jeff got a great jump on the ball but didn't get his glove down far enough, and the ball squirted between his legs. By the time he recovered and reached the ball, two runs had been scored. The game was over.

While the winning team and its fans celebrated in a victor's frenzy, Jeff threw down his glove and plopped down on the infield grass, feeling all the pain of the moment. He was humiliated, angry at the ball, and disgusted with himself.

In the midst of the confusion, Jeff's dad made his way through the crowd onto the playing field. When he reached his son, without hesitation, he picked up the glove and sat down on the grass next to Jeff. After a few moments of silence, Jeff's dad threw the glove down and said, "That's got to hurt more than anything in world."

He didn't ask what happened. He didn't try to diminish or deny the pain of the moment. He just shared it. And his response helped Jeff cope with the disappointment. The pain was still crushing. The missed play was still humiliating. But his dad's action helped Jeff realize he didn't have to face the failure alone. That lesson was far more valuable than the victory would have been.

<u>P R I N C I P L E</u>

The first thing parents can do to help their kids learn from their failures is to identify with them and share their pain.

A parent won't always be around when a child is overwhelmed by circumstances. In fact, the older a child gets, the more he is forced to handle defeat on his own. However, a parent still plays a critical role in sharing the pain. Even after the fact, a parent can be instrumental in teaching a child how to respond to defeat.

Frank Baum grew up on a wonderful country estate near Syracuse, New York. He had everything a young boy could hope for. In fact, his parents tried to keep him from any difficulty, and they had the resources to be fairly successful. But a few moments during one normal day changed Frank forever.

Frank was playing in the grainfields, and his imagination had him on a great adventure. Suddenly, without warning, a stranger stood in front of him. The towering figure just stood there, silent. Frank was terrified and ran as fast as he could toward home.

For months Frank relived this event in a recurring nightmare. In the dream this nameless, faceless stranger would chase Frank until finally he would wake up. Frank's imagination had created a real, ongoing fear.

Eventually Frank's parents would help him learn that the frightening, silent stranger was nothing but a harmless scarecrow. And when he did, his fearfulness disappeared, but the memory of that day remained. Later on, when Frank told stories to neighborhood children, that stranger in the field became one of his main characters. And eventually those stories were woven into the classic *The Wonderful Wizard of Oz*.[1]

PRINCIPLE

Parents can help kids recover from failure
by helping them put all the facts
into proper perspective.

WHEN PARENTS FAIL

As difficult as it may be to deal with our children's failures, it is far more difficult to have to handle our own failures, as seen through our children's eyes. Life is a risky adventure, and we will make mistakes. There are no perfect parents, and it wouldn't be good if there were. If we were perfect, how would our kids learn to handle their own failures and why would they need God? We can make a lasting impression on our kids as we find the up side to our own failures, even our failures in raising our children.

As I was talking about this principle with one of my close friends, he volunteered his experience with trying to be perfect. He said, "When our first child was born, my wife and I were obsessed with being perfect parents. We were going to do everything right. That was a miserable time. Now, after three kids, if we get through the day and everyone is healthy and functioning, it's time to celebrate. Now we are more relaxed and we really enjoy our kids. We had to give ourselves the freedom to fail."

In *Newsweek*, staff writer James Sheehy told of watching his son demonstrate his skateboarding skills. A burst of youthfulness came over Sheehy, and he began to imagine himself zipping around on that skateboard.

"Yo! Dad!" his son called. "Come on. It's fun. You just get on it and go."

After a moment of courage gathering Sheehy agreed, and with the help of his son he stood up on the board.

"Now," his son said, "make it move."

Sheehy kept one foot on the board and pushed with the other until he got to the downhill slope of the driveway. The rest is a blur. The board shot out from under him, and he went flying through the air, landing with his full weight on the side of one foot.

"Wow, Dad! That was radical. Do it again," his son cheered.

On the way to the hospital the son retold every detail of the flying skateboard ride. He told everyone in the emergency room how neat it was.

When the doctor walked up, he took one look at the foot and responded rather critically, "Riding a skateboard at your age..."[2]

Sheehy was spending time with his son—sharing his interests, sharing the fun, and allowing his son to be the expert and he the student. If we are too afraid of failing, we will take too little action. If, however, we are willing to risk failing in front of our kids, and can laugh when we do fail, we teach them to have the courage to try new things and not to be devastated or defensive when there are problems. Learning to laugh at our own mistakes is one of the greatest lessons in life—a lesson we teach best by example.

P R I N C I P L E

Parents can help kids recover from their failures by being willing to risk failure themselves and by accepting it with a bit of humor when it comes.

We can empathize with the pain of failure. We can help our children put it in perspective. We can model willingness to risk failure and handling it with grace and humor, thereby minimizing the fear and pain of failure. But we also need to help our children take responsibility for changing those things within their control that lead to failure. Sometimes a course correction is necessary.

When Michele was in grade school, she was really lonely, and she compensated by eating all the wrong food. As the fat accumulated, so did her misery. Her dad added to the problem by calling her uncomplimentary nicknames.

In the middle of Michele's seventh grade year there was to be a banquet at school. Her mother borrowed an almost new dress for Michele from a cousin, but Michele hated the dress, her pudgy body, and having to go to the banquet. So she announced she wasn't going.

After taking a second look at her pain, her wise and repentant father gave her a present she never forgot. Michele's dad spent the afternoon at the mall, going from store to store, searching for just the right dress for his daughter. He found two, and since he couldn't decide which was best, he bought both.

When her dad handed her the boxes, Michele couldn't believe her eyes. She opened the first, and out sprang a beautiful black formal. And in the second was a hot pink semi-formal dress. Suddenly the room was full of white tissue, tears, and hope.[3]

Dad's renewed awareness of his daughter's feelings made it possible to recover from a failure that would have had lasting impact. From that day forward the uncomplimentary nicknames were never heard.

P R I N C I P L E

Parents help kids grow from failure by taking responsibility for changing the things that can and need to be changed.

TWO-SIDED LESSONS

Failures of any kind are difficult to accept and to recover from, but they are especially difficult to handle when we realize we were irresponsible or when we broke the rules. We don't like to admit our guilt, but when we do, we discover the power of confession and forgiveness. And we discover the up side of failure. At these times we have the opportunity to make a lasting impression on our children by modeling the appropriate action.

Confession

Charlie found out about confession firsthand.

On Saturday Charlie's family could have peanut brittle any time they wanted, all day. But Saturday was the only day candy was allowed in the house. The rule was the same for children and adults.

Charlie was up late one Friday night, watching TV, when he got a craving for peanut brittle. He knew where the candy was, and he knew how to get into the package without being caught. Everyone was asleep; no one would know. Besides, he was the one who had made up the rule in the first place, and in just one hour it would be Saturday anyway.

So he broke into the peanut brittle and enjoyed every bite. The next day everything went fine; no one even suspected. But Charlie began to feel guilty. He decided to tell his family what he had done—to confess. But he would wait for just the right time.

That night after dinner, just when Charlie was about to begin his confession, Charlie's wife announced she couldn't find the cake she had made for dessert. "Can you believe it? A whole cake just disappeared!"

She asked Randy about the cake, and he complained that he always got the blame. "No," he replied, "I didn't take your cake!"

She asked six-year-old Christy, and Christy responded, "No, Mom. Jesus wouldn't want me to take the cake."

Charlie decided this was not the time for a peanut brittle confession.

Mom decided that the twins across the street must have taken the cake. After all, they never knocked when they came in, and they would go directly to the refrigerator and help themselves.

That night Charlie and his wife were having a little tiff. The timing was still wrong.

Tuesday was the night. The family gathered in Christy's room to say a bedtime prayer, and after the prayer Charlie asked everyone to stay seated for a bit. "Last Friday night," Charlie began, "I broke into the peanut brittle, and I am feeling really guilty. I am sorry, and I want you to forgive me."

As soon as Charlie finished, Christy reached down under the bed and pulled out what was left of the cake. She explained, "Dad, you know the new family that moved in down the street? Well, Saturday was the boy's birthday. The parents were too busy for a party, so the twins wrapped up some old toys and I brought the cake. I thought we would only eat a few pieces and then I could squeeze the cake back together, but we ate too much. When I tried to squeeze it back up, it all crumbled. So I hid it under my bed, and I snack on it at night. I'm sorry, Mom. But, Dad," she continued, "when you told about the peanut brittle, I had to tell about the cake."

Confession can work miracles. I have seen parental confession of failure have a dramatic, turnaround impact on confused kids. But, by all accounts, it is the rarest of parent-child memories.

P R I N C I P L E

Parents help kids learn from failure by modeling how and when to confess their mistakes.

Forgiveness

The natural response to confession is forgiveness. All of God's children remember that wonderful, fresh-start feeling that accompanies forgiveness. After twenty-five years of working with families of all types, I am convinced that the number one priority of parents seeking to raise spiritually strong children should be forgiveness.

Two wonderful things happen when parents and kids experience a confession-forgiveness time. The kids learn how to forgive others, and they end up with a deeper sense of family loyalty. As children learn to forgive within the family, they are also better prepared to forgive the failures of others as they extend their boundaries beyond the home.

During a lunch break at a Family Conference in Dallas, Texas, Bob told me his tragic story of failure and forgiveness.

Bob's dad had an automatic pistol that Bob loved. By the time Bob was thirteen, his dad had taken him to the firing range enough for him to feel confident handling the gun. But every time they returned from the range, Bob's dad would tell him never, under any circumstances, to touch the pistol unless he was with him.

One day, just to show off in front of his friends, Bob got the gun and with the help of his buddies did a little target practicing in the backyard.

Darlene, a nine-year-old girl who lived two houses down the street, was watching from just inside the gate. When Bob finished firing at the targets, he turned to scare her. Thinking the gun was empty, he waved it at her and pulled the trigger. The gun fired. There was one shell left. Bob went into hysterics.

That beautiful little girl fell to the ground and died two hours later. Bob was devastated. He didn't want to see anyone. He stayed in his room for days. Virtually everyone in town attended Darlene's funeral but Bob.

The morning after the funeral, her older brother, who was twenty-six at the time, came to see Bob. He walked into Bob's room and said, "Come with me. I'm taking you to school." That was the last place Bob wanted to be, but he was not given a choice.

Darlene's brother didn't say much on the way. When they arrived at school, he took Bob to the principal's office where he somehow talked the principal into calling the entire student body together for an assembly.

As soon as all 580 students were in their places, Darlene's brother took the microphone and began his speech. "A terrible thing has happened; my little sister has been killed. She was accidentally shot by one of your classmates. We will all miss Darlene, but I want you to do something for her family today."

Then he motioned for Bob to come up on stage. While Bob struggled to put one foot in front of the other, the brother continued talking. "Yesterday our family and Bob's family met with our minister, and we gave this tragedy to God." Then he put his arm around Bob and said, "This boy's future depends on us and our willingness to forgive him. Darlene would want us to do that. So I ask you not to judge Bob on his failures, not to talk about this tragedy behind his back, and to accept him back as a friend—a friend who has made a terrible mistake, but still a friend."

Then everyone walked out together, and a burden was lifted from Bob's shoulders. He still had to live with the memory of that senseless action, but because of Darlene's brother, he began to feel the redeeming power of forgiveness.

Bob concluded his story by saying, "I have two vivid memories of that tragedy—the sound of the gun firing and the words of forgiveness."

PRINCIPLE

*Parents help kids learn that forgiveness
doesn't take away the consequences or the memory,
but it does give us hope.*

In *A Gift of Hope* author Robert Veninga tells about one of the most traumatic realities a parent could ever face. Allen Comstock didn't see his four-year-old son when he backed the family station wagon out of the driveway. Although the boy survived, he was left with a permanent limp, and Allen was left with the guilt.

As the boy grew older, Allen would go to hockey games with his son. But they were painful reminders that the accident had kept his boy from skating and doing all the normal things kids do. They would go to the beach, and Allen would see the ugly scars on his boy's leg, and he would turn away in tears. When his son started dating, Allen could see how hesitant he was, and Allen just knew it was because of the stiff leg. But as the son grew into his midteens, Allen began to realize his boy was going to make it. He had a girlfriend. He received a scholarship to the University of Kentucky. He was doing great. But Allen was miserable and depressed.

Then one day as the two were driving along in the car, for the first time Allen's son asked about the details of the accident. It was the one question Allen had feared for years.

Allen says, "I told him everything that occurred and even how the passing years had not taken away the feelings of being responsible. And you know what my kid did? He put his hand on my shoulder and said: 'I never blamed you for what happened. I never thought of it as your fault.'"[4]

That night Allen wept, but they were tears of relief. For the first time in thirteen years, he went to bed without the load of guilt. Acceptance had been there all along, just for the asking.

P R I N C I P L E

Parents help kids learn that the greatest failure comes from trying to hide the guilt and deny the pain.

Our parents' examples and expectations have a powerful impact on us, even long after we have left home. In the middle of the Watergate hearings the voice Charles Colson was listening to was his father's. Colson tells of being on the witness stand and flashing back to Sunday afternoons with his father. He could hear his father say, "There is nothing more important than telling the truth. Always tell the truth." Then Colson says, "I took a few deep breaths, sat up straight in my chair, and gave truthful answers. I did the same thing the forty-four other times I was called to testify under oath during Watergate."

Colson continues, "My father died while I was prison,...but I think he experienced the same peace I did. As I was being sentenced, his question was, 'Have you told the truth?' I told him I had. He looked at me with a confident smile. 'Then you'll be all right.' And he was right."[5]

Being truthful is a prerequisite for handling failure. First, we must be honest with ourselves. Second, we must be honest with those around us. We can't fix any failure without it.

P R I N C I P L E

By their early teaching, parents will continue to help their children learn from their failures long after they have left home.

To find the up side of a failure requires taking responsibility for our part of what has happened. Then, instead of thinking "if only," think "next time." "If only" keeps us focused on the past and the failure, while "next time" directs us to what we will do or say in the future. "Next time" is a subtle reminder that we have learned something in the midst of our pain.

P R I N C I P L E

"Next time" is a great lead-in for parents to use with their kids so that discussions about failuress focus on what can be learned and what can be improved when problems recur.

As the story goes, Babe Ruth was playing one of the last games of his career, and he had struck out each time at the plate. His body just wasn't able to play the game quite like it had in his younger days.

He was playing right field. It was the last of the ninth. There were two outs with a runner on second. The score was tied. The ball was hit sharply just to his left. Ruth fielded the ball well, but his throw to third was wild, bouncing over the third baseman's head and allowing the winning run to be scored. The game was over.

The crowd erupted in boos and jeers. They blamed Ruth for the loss, and they were much wilder than his throw had been. No one needed to make Ruth feel bad; he would have booed himself, but nobody could have heard.

While the crowd was focused on Ruth, a little blond-headed boy jumped down onto the top of the dugout and then down onto the field. As he ran out toward Ruth, a hush fell over the crowd. He jumped up into Babe Ruth's arms, and then hand in hand they walked toward the dugout. By then the crowd was totally silent.

Later one reporter explained the silence by saying, "The crowd was watching the love of a little boy for his hero, even when his hero failed."

Our first step as parents is to demonstrate the same kind of love this little boy had for his hero. Whatever the failure, we are to give our unconditional love, just as our spiritual father does.

When Children Fail

In relationship to God: Pray for God to help your kids know they don't have to be perfect to be loved, and for God to help you learn to let them fail.

In relationship to your children: Identifying with the pain is best accomplished without questions and with very few words. Statements like "That's gotta hurt!" are helpful. Then turn on your ears and listen. Listen with your eyes, with your hugs, and with your heart. No criticism allowed.

When Parents Fail

In relationship to God: Ask God to help you feel more comfortable admitting your failures to your children and to him.

In relationship to your children: Tell your kids about a time when you failed. Tell what helped you deal with the failure and what you learned through your failure.

Two-sided Lessons

In relationship to God: Ask God to help you teach your kids how to confess and forgive.

In relationship to your children: Select a special place in or around your home to become your Confession and Forgiveness Center. Make that place a family secret. Invite the family to gather there and ask each one to finish the following sentence: "Forgiveness is...." Use this discussion to introduce your center. Make it your place for total openness.

STEP ONE

In relationship to God: Seek the Lord's help in knowing how to share the feelings that come from failure. Ask him to help you see with your heart.

In relationship to your children: Plan a "We Messed Up Celebration." Make it a festive atmosphere. Ask each person to share a mess-up and how he or she felt. Then share a messed up cake. (Use your imagination to make a mess of the cake.) This could easily become an annual event at your house.

Chapter Five

KIDS NEVER FORGET THE MILESTONES OF GROWING UP

I n Kenya, young Obi is kidnapped by a group of hooded
men who are swinging sticks and beating drums. A similar hood is slipped over his head, his hands are tied, and
he's led away to some distant place where he will complete his
rite of passage into adulthood. During the next few weeks he
will be tested to see if he can survive the trek from the distant,
secret, manhood-hut back to his home. While he is on his journey, his parents mourn the boy who will be no more, and they
celebrate the man who will return.

We label this practice primitive, but it provides for both the
child and the parents in that society a vivid and unforgettable
milestone. Countries around the world have different ways of
marking this passage—everything from clipping the earlobes,
to passing a ritual test of character, to engaging in mortal com-
bat.

But in America we have no single milestone. American families don't cut the cord all at once; we cut it one strand at a time.

We have developed a grab bag of unofficial milestones scattered throughout childhood and adolescence. Although not any one of them is as sensational as being kidnapped, each of our unofficial milestones is significant, and as they are stacked together, they consciously or unconsciously force us to grow up.

Growing up implies a gradual expansion of our world and our place in it, but once in a while this process takes a jump step, and milestones are passed. With each milestone children move a little closer to adulthood, and life gets more understandable, more independent, and more complex.

Some milestones have structured, public impact, while others are more private and vary from child to child. Regardless of whether the milestone is public or private, parents play a major role. We need to prepare our children for the milestones of adulthood and to celebrate each new level of maturity when it occurs. And at each milestone parents are called on to cut a connecting strand—to release a bit of our hold—an experience we need just as much as our children do.

EXPANDING WORLDS

The first series of milestones children face expands their physical world. To begin with, the child's physical territory is limited to the crib, the room, the house, the yard, and the neighborhood. Sometime during childhood, children begin creating their own space within these confines of home. This space becomes a territorial milestone, a little step toward adulthood.

Personal Space

During the summer I was six, my dad bought five dozen, eight-foot, four by four, redwood posts to build a fence around our apricot trees. The fence was never built, but my buddies and I spent years shaping that stack of posts into the most creative forts, clubhouses, and sailing vessels ever built in northern California.

A young mother in Houston told me how her creative eight-year-old constructed a tent for a campout. "Well, it wasn't really a tent," she said. "It was a collection of blankets strung over ropes tied to the patio posts. And it wasn't really outside; it was under the covered patio with extension cords giving light and power to the tiny fort. And they didn't really sleep; they told scary stories, ate junk food, laughed, and kept running into the house for one more thing. They managed to successfully transfer the contents of three rooms into the carefully arranged space under the blankets. It took a week to find everything and return it to the proper place."

P R I N C I P L E

Personal space milestones are marked by kids using make-believe and play to take their first steps toward independence.
Parents can help by encouraging their children to discover a personal space just right for them.

Sleepovers

Another milestone for American children is the sleepover. Sleepovers take us just beyond the protective arms of our parents and test our spirit of adventure.

I was sitting across from Christopher, a robust five-year-old. He had spent the night at his buddy's house, and I was curious how it went.

"What did you do?"

"Watched *Ducktales*," he responded. "Ate dinner. Played outside. Went to bed. Got up and here I am."

His outline seemed so matter-of-fact, I doubted that he'd had a good time. "What was the best part?" I asked.

"The food. We had pizza. I ate four pieces."

Like Christopher, children may remember some detail of a sleepover, like the food or a scary moment or a game that was played, but the sleepover is a milestone because it expands the circle of security beyond the home, and with it the child takes small steps toward independence.

P R I N C I P L E
_____

*The sleepover milestone helps kids expand their feelings
of security to another home.*

First Day of School

The physical territory for a child changes dramatically when the child begins school. School forces him into new challenges, new relationships, new opportunities, and new choices. The first day of school is one of the most identifiable milestones in the life of the child and the parent. Just as children begin the first day of school with mixed feelings, so do parents. For many parents this milestone is one of the toughest. That's why we can't wait for the child to get home so we can play "Twenty Questions"—or why we go to school with them, just in case.

Author Barbara Jean Rinkoff captures the stress and joy of this milestone in her book *Rutherford T Finds 21B*. Rutherford T is dressed and ready for his first day at school. His mother, who has to stay home with the new baby, tries to comfort Rutherford by telling him he will soon make many new friends. Rutherford isn't so sure. On the way to school he whispers his name and room number to himself so he won't forget.

Once at school he begins looking for his room. Because he can't read the numbers, Rutherford asks for help. He asks the first boy he meets how to get to 21B, and the two of them search together. They ask another student, and another, and another. Rutherford quickly becomes friends with each child who tries to help him. Eventually the children find Rutherford's classroom, and once in his room Rutherford realizes that his mother was right—he has already made a lot of new friends.[1]

Encouraging our kids to talk about this new "school world" will help us release them with more joy and confidence. And these early discussions will set a pattern of sharing our daily adventures with each other.

P R I N C I P L E

The school milestone prepares kids to test the view of life they have learned from their parents.
It helps parents to switch from solving their children's problems to encouraging their children to solve them.

Adventures beyond Adult Eyes

Getting to play beyond the eyes of adults is a significant step for most kids. It is, however, a milestone being threatened by the violent and abusive atmosphere in many sections of our country. I was blessed to grow up across the street from a two-hundred-acre park that others called Alvarado Park. I called it and claimed it mine.

This eucalyptus-treed hillside was crisscrossed by equestrian trails connecting cookout areas, playgrounds, a roller-skating rink, and lots of secret hiding places. In the shallow waters of Wildcat Creek I discovered what tadpoles taste like, found lost socks, and learned you can't swim in twelve inches of water.

At the roller-skating rink I learned the hokey-pokey. On the hillside I learned how much fun it could be to slide down on an old piece of cardboard—and how horrible it could be to slide through poison oak.

Playing across the street was my testing ground for independence. The whole park was my own world, and it was there that I led great adventures, discovered buried treasure, and escaped the pain of an alcoholic father. My mother realized that I needed lots of "across the street" time, and she allowed me that freedom.

P R I N C I P L E

Allow kids some freedom to explore beyond their home as they prove their responsibility with time, property, rules, and behavior.

Taking the Car

When I ask young adults about the milestones of their lives, they always mention something about driving—getting their license, taking the car solo for the first time, or getting their first car. For teenagers the car is an unmistakable symbol of freedom. It is a major expansion of their world.

I remember the first time I got to take the car by myself. I felt so grown up.

Our youth group always attended the monthly church skating party, and for the first time I got to drive. I loaded ten kids into our 1960 Ford station wagon, and with this young, but confident, sixteen-year-old driving, we headed off on the thirty-minute trip to the skating rink.

The trip to the rink was uneventful. The skating was uneventful. But not so the trip home.

Feeling adventurous, I decided to go home on the back road—a narrow, two-lane, winding road with little traffic and no shoulder. About halfway home I rounded a corner and hit the biggest chuckhole in California. The right front tire blew instantly. I pulled the car safely to a stop, but since there was no shoulder, we had to change the tire in the middle of the road.

While Russell and Tim tried to light the flares (which no one had ever done before), Brian tried to operate the jack (which took fifteen minutes to find and twenty more to work) and I searched for a flashlight (which I never found). After more than an hour of stumbling around in the dark, the flat was changed, and we were on our way again. We never saw a single car on that road that night.

The next morning I told my dad about the blowout, and we looked at the tire. It was destroyed, and the wheel was bent in two inches.

I took a jump step toward adulthood that night. From that flat tire forward, safety was my first thought instead of an afterthought. I was fortunate; I got to learn a lesson in responsibility without getting hurt.

P R I N C I P L E

To a teenager, a car is not just transportation,
it's independence.
Parents need to give access to the car a little at a time.

First Paycheck

That first real job—part-time or full-time—when somebody pays you real money is a personal milestone. In America, getting a regular paycheck is considered by many to be the final marker of adulthood. It definitely changes our world.

One young man visiting at our house told me, "I start training next week! I can't believe it. I have a job! I went into that store a kid, and I came out with a whole new identity!"

P R I N C I P L E

The primary significance of the job milestone is not the money but the experience of trying out a new identity.

Trips with Friends

Independent trips or outings with friends can become private milestones that allow the adolescent to take further steps toward being an adult. These trips give limited adventures of independence.

A few months ago several of us were gathered around a blazing fire in the fireplace, sharing stories of growing up. I'll never forget Ed's story.

> There were five of us that were always together. We had been best friends since grade school. As our high school graduation gift, our parents had joined forces and had given us the money for a twenty-one day trip across the country. The day after graduation we took off. My dad actually let five, seventeen-year-old boys take his Suburban for the seventy-five hundred mile trip. He must have been unconscious.
>
> We had planned for weeks. Nothing could go wrong.
>
> At our first stop Jeff left our detailed map in the rest room of the 7-11 store. That was okay. We were grown men; we didn't need the map. Russell said he knew a shortcut. His shortcut put us three hours behind schedule.

After a late dinner we bought another map and decided to spend the night driving down the road under the stars. Without warning, we heard a loud phsssssss, and the air conditioning stopped immediately. So down came the windows. A sudden gust of wind blew our newly acquired map out the side window. Again we were lost. But we were men, so we kept going.

Sharon, Jack's girlfriend, had given him some brownies to share with everyone, but he had kept them all for himself. He had eaten three before he noticed he had a problem; he needed to use the bathroom—fast. It was then we discovered a note from Sharon. She had laced the brownies with a laxative, as a joke. Everyone laughed but Jack.

By eleven o'clock we were hot, hungry, lost, and tired. I pulled off the highway onto a remote road and stopped for the night. It was pitch dark, so we used the lights from the Suburban to see where to lay our sleeping bags. Within a half-hour we were all asleep, except Jack.

At 3:14 A.M. I woke up to loud rumblings. Before I could get to the Suburban's lights, a bright light flashed ahead of us and was headed straight for us. We all scrambled in major panic. I was sure the Suburban was toast.

Russell yelled, "Beam me up, Scotty!"

Jack, who was having trouble moving fast, yelled, "It's a train!"

It was just then that the train turned and stormed by, within a few feet of the Suburban. We were parked five feet from the tracks and didn't know it.

Did that trip work out the way they had planned it? Nothing happened as planned! Will they ever forget it? Not a chance. It became a milestone journey, an initiation, and they returned understanding a little more about life as adults.

P R I N C I P L E

The trip milestone is a concentrated test of freedom and responsibility. Passing it gives parents and teens a new level of confidence.

EXPLORING NEW FEELINGS

Some milestones don't explore new worlds, but new feelings. They are more private, and parents may or may not even be aware of them, but they are just as important. Private milestones help pave the way for some of the public ones. Kids need these experiences to build confidence and courage for the risky task of growing up, but even supportive and understanding parents may find these private milestones especially frustrating.

Forbidden Words

I love the youngster who grabbed his coat and boots and asked, "Mom, can I go outside and help Dad put the snow chains on the tires? I know all the right words." Somewhere along the line this young boy had heard the curse words and the "four-letter" words and felt that he too could now talk like an adult.

Do you remember when you learned the "adult words" and what they meant? Getting to know these forbidden words seems to be a milestone event for most youngsters. Just becoming aware of the words is far more important than using them.

When I was in graduate school working in the Child Development Center, I remember overhearing a debate between two five-year-olds on which four-letter word was the worst. After much discussion, they decided that the "F" word was the worst because it got the loudest reaction from their parents. Just knowing the words signals a new stage of childhood and new feelings about growing up. With the influence and accessibility of television, this language awareness milestone is, unfortunately, reached all too early.

P R I N C I P L E

It helps if parents learn to be shockproof.
This will allow parents to turn four-letter words
into family talks.

Daydreams

For most children daydreams are a wonderful diversion. And for some, they provide an escape from the painfulness of reality.

When we were younger, many of us dreamed about bravely saving our family from some disaster, beating the school bully at his own game, making the fifty-foot, winning shot as the buzzer sounded in toughest basketball game of the year, dating the most popular student at school, or getting an *A* on a geometry test. Our daydreams tested the connection between our emotions and our will. They become emotional milestones.

P R I N C I P L E

This milestone helps kids develop their "what if"
thinking ability—problem-solving.
Parents can help by viewing daydreaming
as a mental exercise, not as laziness.

The Crush

First love is unforgettable. In fact the "first love" feelings are so intense that, at that moment, we are not sure anyone has ever experienced love the way we are experiencing it.

Phyllis Reynolds Naylor paints a marvelous portrait of a young teenager named Alice experiencing her first love. Her summer between grade school and junior high is filled with ball games, bike riding, and the first "crush."

First signs of the summer "crush" come via the telephone. Patrick's on the phone:

> "What are you doing?" he asked.
>
> "Nothing much," I said. "What are *you* doing?"...
>
> "Do you want me to come over?" Patrick asked.
>
> "Do *you* want to?" I said.
>
> "If you want me to," he answered.
>
> "I do if you do," I told him....
>
> "Okay, I'll come over," said Patrick, and hung up.
>
> I rushed upstairs and brushed my teeth, changed my T-shirt, combed my hair, and put on a pair of sandals. Then I sat down on the couch again, mussed up my hair a little, pulled on my T-shirt to make it look baggy, and kicked off one sandal so it would look as though I hadn't even moved since he'd called.[2]

P R I N C I P L E

The crush milestone opens the child's world of
"love," infatuation, and risk taking.
If parents are sensitive, they can be great
sounding boards during this time.

Puberty

This milestone drains the patience of both the young teen and the parents. Living with a body that takes years to develop and a social agenda that wants everything now can create no small amount of stress, frustration, and worry. "Children fret, teenagers worry," says David Elkind, popular child development specialist. "Children fret about what they can and cannot have, where they can and cannot go. Teenagers worry about themselves, about what they will look like once they pass through puberty, about the future."[3] We did the same thing.

During puberty teenagers develop into world-class worriers:

Girls worry if they will ever get their period.

Boys worry about being too short.

Both worry that there is a right way to kiss and they don't know it.

Girls worry that their breasts are too round, or too pointed, or too flat.

Boys worry that they'll get breasts.

Both worry that someone will hear them going to the bathroom or that the lock on the door won't work.

Girls worry about their weight and shape.

Boys worry about a spontaneous erection during math class.

Both worry about controlling their sexual impulses.

Girls worry about their skin.

Boys worry about getting hair in the right places.

Both worry that they won't be just like their friends.

During this time of life kids are extremely self-conscious and self-focused. They are concerned that everyone is watching them and that everyone knows they feel self-conscious. And, at times they have no idea how they feel. With the invasion of testosterone and estrogen, things are happening emotionally and physically that teens don't understand. (Nor do we.) The changes are beyond their control, and there is no way of knowing how they will turn out. The teen is supersensitive, and the heightened emotions set the stage for strong memories, both good and bad.

PRINCIPLE

*The puberty milestone puts kids on
an emotional roller coaster. Parents can reduce the stress
by injecting humor, keeping communication open,
and taking life one day at a time.*

DEVELOPING SPIRITUAL CONVICTIONS

Questioning

Searching for answers to the tough "why" questions becomes a spiritual milestone only when the search is personally motivated. Just participating in a philosophical discussion is not a milestone. Only when the person himself or herself is asking serious questions does it become a milestone of spiritual growth.

Recently I overheard the following dialogue:

Mom: Brenda, do you believe in God?

Brenda (age 14): That's a rather personal question.

Mom: You're right, but I'm just curious. I'd really like to know.

Brenda: I guess. But do you remember last year when Mrs. Filbeck, down the street, was in the hospital and we all prayed for her to get well and she didn't? Well, six months ago I asked

God to help a friend who was really struggling with drugs, and God didn't do anything. Then this week I asked God for help on my French test, and I got a *D*. I believe in God, but I sure don't understand him.

P R I N C I P L E

The questioning milestone is a necessary step in developing a strong personal faith. Kids who are at this milestone should be taken seriously.

Parents can help kids through this milestone by being open about their own questions and by realizing that questioning is an important step in developing personal convictions.

Turning Convictions to Commitment

The mysterious moment of conversion has a double impact on young people. They are freed from the guilt of their past, and they are accepted into God's family. Within this conversion milestone is the potential for a total remake of life.

On my eleventh birthday I decided it was time to commit my life to God and be baptized. I wanted God to know how much I loved him, so I responded to the altar call, told the preacher about my decision, and away we went to the changing room. There he told me to take off my clothes and put on the white things hanging on the hook.

When I came out, he opened the locked doors that led into the baptistry. A spider, some bugs, and scum floated on the surface of the water. Like a modern-day Moses, he roughed up the water, and miraculously the yucky stuff disappeared. Then we both walked down into the water. As the preacher talked to me about what was going to happen, I searched for the return of those bugs.

I knew the angels in heaven were going to rejoice when I got baptized. That's what the Bible says, right? In fact, I expected to hear them. Once the curtain was pulled the preacher began a second sermon. (I think he got started and didn't know how to stop.) At just the right time he pushed me under, and as soon as I came up, I listened for the angels' singing. Instead, what I heard was the church dragging an old song all the way across the state—"Oh, happy…day,…Oh happy…day when…Jesus…washed…my…sins…away…."

They definitely were not angels.

PRINCIPLE

The spiritual commitment milestone helps kids demonstrate their love for God in a personal and public way.
This milestone challenges parents to re-examine their own spiritual journey and personal commitment.

Youth Group

In February 1991 the Center for Adolescent Studies in Abilene, Texas, released the results of a comprehensive national study of spirituality among church teens in America. The fundamental question was "What helps our adolescents take God seriously in their lives?"

One of the survey questions caught my attention: "What events have helped you grow spiritually?" From the more than twenty-five hundred teens who responded, these were the top three events:

1. Summer mission trips

2. Summer camps

3. Youth retreats

Teens remember the times when they pull away from their

everyday world, get together with other kids, and focus on life beyond their immediate concerns. Since these experiences seem to be the most memorable of all the youth group activities, encourage your teens to participate in them.

P R I N C I P L E

*This milestone helps kids realize
how much they need other Christians and God.
It helps parents accept the role of other adults in
the spiritual growth of their children.*

WHERE DO WE BEGIN?

One of the dangers of milestones is the possibility of kids rushing into them before they are ready. Kids may get impatient to have greater freedom, to be grown-up, to have more privileges, and they may end up pushing milestones prematurely. Parents also, out of their own ego needs or lack of awareness, may pressure kids to grow up too soon. Every child has a unique maturity schedule, a genetic timetable, that can be nurtured, but it must be allowed to occur naturally. If we try to push our kids too quickly from milestone to milestone, we put them at risk of trying to handle situations before they are equipped for them. Take Rocco Morabito for example.

At 7 A.M. on Friday, December 4, 1987, Rocco took his mother's car keys, picked up his baby sister, opened the garage door, backed out the family station wagon, and took off down Midland Avenue in Port Chester, New York, in rush-hour traffic. Two-and-a-half miles from home, Rocco was pulled over by a local policeman. The car had violated no laws; it was just that the policeman couldn't see any driver. When the officer walked up, he spotted Rocco, clad in pajamas and sneakers, and his sister, clad only in a pajama top.

Rocco was five. His mother was home sick, his father was at work, so Rocco had set off on his own.

When the officer told Rocco his mother would have to come get him, the kid replied, "My mommy can't come here, because I have the only car. I can drive. I'll go get her."[4]

Rocco had rushed a milestone, fortunately with no serious repercussions. However, that is often not the case.

One compassionate old man witnessed a butterfly struggling to emerge from its cocoon. It appeared that without help the young winged creature was doomed to die. So the old man took out his pocket knife and gingerly slit open the cocoon.

The opening allowed the butterfly to slip away from the cocoon, but something was wrong. The struggle with the cocoon was necessary to give the butterfly's wings time to dry; without the struggle the wings were useless. Now the old man could do nothing but watch the fragile creature die. The beautiful butterfly was free from the cocoon, but he died never knowing what it was like to fly. The man's good intentions actually denied the young butterfly its life.

Milestones are those points at which our children venture forth a step farther beyond the safe cocoon of home and family. Each milestone leaves children a little wiser, a little stronger, and a bit more prepared to fly on their own. The wise parent will prepare their children for these milestones, will recognize them when they come, will celebrate with the children each new stage of their journey into adulthood, and will treat their kids differently as they progress.

Expanding Worlds

In relationship to God: Ask God to help you have a positive attitude about the milestones your child passes so you can celebrate each one wholeheartedly.

In relationship to your children: Plan a day each year to be your Milestone Review Day. New Year's Eve or New Year's Day might be a place to start. On that day gather the family and show pictures you have taken of the milestone events during the past year. Let each child tell about the milestones and what he or she remembers. Then put all the pictures and any other mementos into a milestone memory box.

Exploring New Feelings

In relationship to God: Pray that God will help you learn to be more confident in sharing your milestone experiences with your children.

In relationship to your children: Schedule a long walk with your child so you can talk about your milestones from the "olden days." Perhaps one-on-one dinner times or overnight trips would fit your family better. The important thing is that your child hears about your milestone events firsthand.

Developing Spiritual Convictions

In relationship to God: Ask God to help you know the right time and place to tell your children about your faith journey.

In relationship to your children: Regularly invite people to your house who have a faith story they like to tell. After dinner or snacks ask them to share their story, and encourage your kids to ask any questions they'd like.

In relationship to God: Ask God for the courage to cut the strands that need to be cut, when they need to be cut.

In relationship to your children: Remember, it's easier to cut the cord one strand at a time than all at once. Make yourself a promise to be more aware of milestone times and your responsibility during those times. Start where you are and take each child one step at a time.

Chapter Six

KIDS NEVER FORGET THE RULES

I n 1991 Ricky Van Shelton took a song written by Russell Smith and Kathy Louvin and pulled the heartstrings of parents across America. The song, titled "Keep it between the Lines," paints a nostalgic picture of a father teaching his youngster a little about driving a car and a lot about life.

I'm right here beside you and you're gonna do fine.
All you got to do is keep it between the lines.
Keep your hands on the wheel.
Believe in the things that are real.
Take your time and keep it between the lines.[1]

Traveling the road of life without lines seems to be the chosen path of a generation of parents who have traded what they perceive to be the confinement of the lines for unavoidable risks in living without lines.

In his address to the 1987 graduating class at Duke University, Ted Koppel put it on the line, so to speak. He suggested that the Ten Commandments would be wonderful lines to stay between: "What Moses brought down from Mt. Sinai were not the Ten Suggestions. They are commandments. Are, not were. The sheer brilliance of the Ten Commandments is that they codify in a handful of words acceptable human behavior, not just for then or now, but for all time."[2]

HOMEWORK FOR PARENTS

For the Christian, the Bible itself becomes the guide for what we believe, how we behave, and how we treat other people. God's commands form the outline of our convictions—the boundary lines for right and wrong. And the task of raising children who live within those lines falls on parents. It is our "homework." The parents who are most successful at raising children who live within God's lines will spend valuable time doing three things:

1. They will model the rules.

2. They will teach the rules.

3. They will enforce the rules.

While we struggle to find the time to do our "homework," our children are soaking up unstated rules and forming their own convictions, whether we're ready or not. They see what rules we live by, and how we enforce rules on them—both stated and unstated ones. Our kids may not obey all the rules in our homes, but they won't forget them. And like us, they will especially remember the ones they pushed against and the ones they broke.

It's time to make modeling, teaching, and enforcing the rules a priority so that our children remember those rules that are truly important. It's time to do our "homework."

MODELING THE RULES

Whether we are aware of it or not, as parents we help our children learn the dos and don'ts everyday. We are a living demonstration of the rules we believe to be important. So our children learn many of our family rules just by watching.

A concerned young mother cornered me at a conference break and shared her story about learning the rules:

> The girls had just moved their playhouse area to the breakfast room, and I noticed how nicely the three preschoolers were playing. I was just about to tell them how pleased I was when the screaming started. Mrs. Robinson, across the street, could have heard my Dena yell, "It's mine! Give it to me. Don't make me scream!"
>
> Until this point Becki, a friend from next door, had been cooperative and compliant, but no longer. She blasted, "No, it's not. It's not yours! I brought it!"
>
> My daughter Sara, the oldest, stood up, folded her arms, and shouted, "All right. Hold it right there, you two. Stop the screaming. I'm the mother, and I'll do the screaming around here."
>
> I stopped in my tracks; for a moment I was speechless. I saw myself in Sara's actions. The folded arms, the shrill voice, and even the words were mine.

"I can laugh about it now," she said, "but at the time I was so preoccupied with house stuff that I wasn't aware of what my children were soaking up. I was modeling the very things I said I'd never do. And the kids were watching more carefully than they were listening."

I couldn't have said it better.

*Parents model rules all the time,
not just when they are consciously trying.
The sights and sounds of home shape convictions
twenty-four hours a day.*

Parents do two things with rules. They use them to protect their children while they're young. And they use them to guide the development of their children's convictions—their preparation for life as responsible adults. The rules that make a difference—that protect and prepare—must be kept by the parents, too. For example, nothing teaches honesty more powerfully than parents who model honesty.

Tom and Pauline Nichter and their eleven-year-old son, Jason, were wandering the mall in Buena Park, California. Tom had been out of work for five months, but the family was surviving.

While on their daily search for food, they found a wallet that contained a $1,500 plane ticket, a wad of hundred dollar bills, and several credit cards. Instead of pocketing the much-needed money, the Nichters took the wallet to a local police station. "We wanted to teach our son, Jason, a lesson about honesty," Mrs. Nichter stated.

The tourist who lost the wallet rewarded them with only a handshake. But after the radio and TV stations and newspapers carried the story, an anonymous well-wisher sent them almost ten thousand dollars, and a local real estate agent offered them six months' free rent in an apartment.

"All we did was what was right," Mrs. Nichter said. "We could have used that money, even just a little of it. But we weren't brought up that way, and we didn't want our son brought up that way."

Police Lt. Patrick Black, whose office took calls and mail for the Nichters, said that they received offers on furniture and numerous job opportunities. A San Diego boy sent Jason a dollar and an ice cream coupon. "Jason was touched by that," Mrs. Nichter said. "Even little children are emptying out their piggy banks for us."[3]

Do you believe Jason Nichter will ever forget the lesson on honesty learned in the spring of 1993?

P R I N C I P L E

*Children "hear" what their parents do
better than what they say.*

TEACHING THE RULES

Our actions may speak louder than our words, but our words can cut deeply. Both discouraging and encouraging words can touch the heart with emotions that last a lifetime, but for over half the kids I interviewed, discouraging words were the only words they remembered hearing.

Frustration Quotes

In our frustration and fatigue we all make discouraging comments that we promised ourselves we would never say. Most of the time these comments reflect our own anger or pain. But when children hear these discouraging comments on a regular basis, they interpret them as rules about themselves and their place in the family. Below are a few of the "frustration quotes" I hear most frequently from children. Beside each quote is a sample of how children hear them as rules about themselves.

Parent's Quote	Child's Rule
How dumb can you get?	I'm not very smart so why try?
You're the sloppiest kid I know.	I'll never be neat enough for mom.
Get out of my face.	I'm less important to Dad than the game he's watching on TV.
You're not leaving the house looking like that.	I'll wear what my parents want when I leave the house and then change on the way.
You don't have the sense you were born with.	I won't tell my parents what I'm doing or what I'm thinking.
I'm wasting my breath.	Lecturing makes parents feel better, like they are in control. Practice not listening.
Don't try that again, Bozo.	Don't get caught next time.
Can't you do anything right?	Don't try anything new at home.
Do you hear me talking to you?	It's time to stop listening.
Watch what you're doing.	I'm a klutz. I don't know how to do anything right.
You'd forget your head if it weren't attached.	I don't have to remember. My parents will do that.

A constant barrage of these discouraging words distorts a child's view of life. As the child perceives the life rules that underlie these words, they can have enormous destructive power. Garrison Keillor provides a vivid description of this power.

Our Sunday School class learned "Joy to the World" for the Christmas program. You asked me to sing it for the aunts and uncles when they came to dinner. I said no. You said yes. I said no. You said, "Someday when I'm dead and in my coffin, maybe you'll look down and remember the times I asked you to do things and you wouldn't." So I sang, terrified of them and terrified about your death. You stopped me halfway through. You said, "Now, come on. You can sing it better than that."

A few years later, when I sang the part of Curly in *Oklahoma!* and everybody else said it was wonderful, you said, "I told him for years he could sing and he wouldn't listen to me."

I did listen to you, that's most of my problem. Everything you said went in one ear and right down my spine. Such as, "You're never going to make anything of yourself."...

Everything I said had hidden meaning for you, even, "I'm going to bed." "You can't even spend a few minutes talking to your parents?" you said....

My every act was a subject of study: "What are you doing?" you asked a million times. "Why didn't you do it before?" (Or "Can't it wait until later?") "Why do it here?" "Why are you so quiet?"...

Now you call me on the phone to ask, "Why don't you ever call us? Why do you shut us out of your life?" So I start to tell you about my life, but you don't want to hear it. You want to know why I didn't call.

I didn't call because I don't need to talk to you anymore. Your voice is in my head, talking constantly from morning till night. I keep the radio on, but I still hear you and will hear you until I die....[4]

This doesn't mean that with one negative comment you have ruined your children forever. Criticisms don't become rules unless they are the primary comments a child hears. Left unchecked, our children will hear the same voices Keillor describes.

P R I N C I P L E

Parents who constantly barrage their children with discouraging criticisms and questions are teaching rules that may limit their children for a lifetime.

Rules to Live By

Becoming a better, more persuasive lecturer is not the answer. In fact, our lectures on the rules often last about as long as the sound of the words. They are perceived as judgments, and judgments are turned off immediately. However, some "words to live by" are remembered and passed down from generation to generation.

I asked the subscribers to *Heart and Home*, a family values newsletter that I edit, to send me examples of the "rules to live by" that they recalled from childhood. The following is a selection of their more colorful "wit and wisdom."

Forget about the mules; just load the wagon.

Look for ways to make others feel important.

Don't ever tell anybody all you know; otherwise, they'll know twice as much as you.

Look people in the eye when you talk to them.

Carry jumper cables in the car.

Take extra pictures of people, and give the extras away.

Be fair and square; learn to share.

Try something new once a week.

Replace "if only" with "next time."

Leave everything a little better than you found it.

Never cut what can be untied.

Don't major in minors.

Always ask: What would Jesus do?

Pray for courage more than things.

Remember, goldfish don't like Jell-O.

Treat people like you want to be treated.

Keep your watch five minutes fast.

Never give up on anybody.

Don't "freeze frame" people.

Motel mattresses are better on the side away from the phone.

Regardless of what else you do with your life, be honest.

Women with two first names usually know how to make terrific peach cobbler.

These "words to live by" make the most memorable impression when they are both taught and modeled by the parents. One subscriber added this note: "Just listing these quotes has brought warm feelings to my heart. For most of them I can remember where we were and what we were doing when I heard the words. Now, when I think of them, I feel reconnected to my mom and dad. I'm still living by those words."

P R I N C I P L E

Parents who reduce their lectures
to a few, succinct principles will have a better chance
of being heard and remembered.

ENFORCING THE RULES

Many of the adults I interviewed reported learning more from the few (who counted?) rules they broke than from the many rules they kept. Perhaps guilt intensified the memory.

Rules are worthless without appropriate consequences for breaking them. This is what discipline is all about—enforcing the rules. Most of us need to be reminded, daily, that discipline should always have a redemptive quality—"What did I learn from this experience?" The goal of all discipline should be to protect our children when they need it, to prepare them for the future, to develop their personal convictions, and to help them live by those convictions.

A young mother in Houston, Texas, remembered:

> I was eleven. It was a hot summer day, and I asked my mother if I could have some lemonade. She said we had no lemons. I said if she gave me the money, I'd go to the store and buy some lemons. She said we had no money to buy lemons.
>
> So I walked to the store—half a mile—stole the lemons and brought them home. I presented them to my mother saying, "Now we can have lemonade."

Mom asked, "Where did you get those lemons?" I told her. I told her I was sorry and that I wouldn't do it again, but it didn't work. She made me walk back by myself, return them, and tell the store owner what I had done.

I'll never forget how I felt. Along with other things, that day I learned that no matter what we lacked, we did not have the right to hurt another person to get it. I never stole again.

PRINCIPLE

Parents who enforce the rules in appropriate and wholesome ways will make lasting, positive impressions on their children.

For some parents, enforcing the rules, following through with the consequences, is the toughest part of their job. For the kids, however, facing the consequences assures the rule will be remembered and taken seriously.

I asked a lunch group to share a time when, as children, they broke a rule and had to pay the price. As they began telling their stories, it was clear that the experiences were extremely vivid. For many there had been a secret thrill in pressing a rule beyond the line and then taking the consequences.

Gary remembered with delight the times he defied the "bedtime, lights out" rule.

For most of my grade school years I was an only child, so I played with my neighborhood buddies as much as possible. Weather permitting, we played baseball or basketball, built forts, took spur-of-the-moment bike adventures, spied on Ramona, who lived in the corner house at the end of the block, and basically just hung out together.

At night, after all the bedtime stuff, I would lie in bed until Mom checked on me and closed the bedroom door. Then I would reach under my bed for my trusty flashlight, hidden up inside the box springs. I would pull the top three or four comic books from the stack on my bedstead, and I was ready for adventure.

I remember pulling the sheet over my head, turning on the flashlight, and reading the adventures of Superman, Batman, and Spiderman—super heroes. I thought the sheet would hide the light, keeping even my most watchful parents in the dark about my late night adventures. It didn't.

When I was caught, my parents took my flashlight, my comics, and my Oreo cookies that were stashed in the pillowcase. I had to go to bed fifteen minutes earlier for a week, and my parents made me read them a story of their choosing each evening. They chose a book called *The Lion, the Witch, and the Wardrobe*.

It was the best punishment I ever had.

If it's true that children often remember the rules they have broken more than the rules they have kept, parents need to keep in mind two important facts. First, there must be clearly defined rules to give structure to the kids' lives. Second, the consequences for breaking the rules need to fit the crime. Two of the most harmful things parents can do are consistently choosing consequences that overkill the crime and, on the other end of the spectrum, constantly rescuing their kids from the consequences of their behavior. Both extremes inhibit the child's development of responsible behavior.

Feeling Forgiven

Holding our children to the consequences of their behavior is important, but so is forgiveness. In fact, forgiveness is one of the most powerful tools a parent has for making lasting memories.

Max Lucado tells a story of the power of forgiveness without even using the word. The story begins in a poor neighborhood on the outskirts of a Brazilian village. Maria and her daughter Christina had struggled through the years following the death of Maria's husband. By age fifteen Christina had developed a spirit of independence much like her mother's. She often talked about traveling to Rio de Janeiro to experience the excitement of city life. The thought of her young daughter trying to live in the big city horrified Maria.

One morning Maria awoke to find her daughter had left for the adventure of the city. The heartbroken mother quickly threw some clothes into a bag, gathered up all her money, and headed to the bus stop. On the way she stopped by the drugstore. There she sat in the photograph booth, closed the curtain, and spent all she could on pictures of herself. With her purse full of small black-and-white photos, she boarded the next bus to Rio.

Maria knew Christina had no money, and she knew her daughter was too stubborn to give up. She knew what her daughter would have to do to earn a living. Maria searched the bars, hotels, nightclubs—any place the street walkers might frequent. At each place she left a picture of herself taped on bathroom mirrors, tacked to hotel bulletin boards, fastened to corners of phone booths. On the back of each photo she wrote a note.

It didn't take long for the money to run out, and Maria was forced to go home, without Christina.

By this time Christina's dream had become a nightmare, and although she longed to be back home, she was too ashamed to take that first step. One day, a few weeks after Maria left Rio, as Christina descended the stairs to the hotel lobby, she noticed a familiar face. There on the lobby mirror was a small picture of her mother. Christina's eyes burned and her throat tightened as she walked across the room and removed the photo. Written on the back was this note: "Whatever you have done, whatever you've become, it doesn't matter. Please come home."

And she did.[5]

That's forgiveness.

PRINCIPLE

Parents who learn how to forgive, even before they are asked, will help their kids forgive themselves and will preserve their relationship.

WHERE DO WE BEGIN?

Children need rules to help them understand what is expected of them. They also need rules to learn the value of justice and the trait of forgiveness. But if we try to have specific rules for everything, the list will be endless. Families must simplify.

In *Teaching Your Children Values*, Linda and Richard Eyre suggest five, one-word rules. You may find them a helpful place to start.

Peace—There is to be no hitting, fighting, yelling, whining, etc.

Pegs—Make a pegboard with three pegs for each child. One peg is for a family job, one is for homework and practicing, and one is for evening tasks like brushing teeth and getting to bed on time. The rule is to get each peg in each day.

Asking—Don't go anywhere or invite anyone over without permission.

Order—Keep your room straight and pick up after yourself.

Obedience—Do what parents say.[6]

Modeling the Rules

In relationship to God: Pray for the courage to keep the rules you want your children to keep, even when they're not looking.

In relationship to your children: Read the story of the Nichters to your family. Ask why they think people responded to the Nichters as they did. Then ask what rules they consider important to keep within your family.

Teaching the Rules

In relationship to God: Ask God to give you opportunities to teach your children your "rules to live by."

In relationship to your children: Become a quotable parent. Make a list of your ten best "rules to live by" and look for opportunities to weave them into your conversations with your kids. As you find yourself facing decision times, quote yourself and live by the rule.

Enforcing the Rules

In relationship to God: Ask God to give you the willpower to follow through with enforcing the rules even when you don't feel like it.

In relationship to your children: List ten rules that tend to get broken in your house. Match an appropriate consequence with each rule. Make sure you don't have any overkills and that you have a variety of consequences. Change whatever needs to be changed. To keep doing the same thing over and over again, expecting different results, doesn't make sense.

Feeling Forgiven

In relationship to God: Pray that God will help you to feel forgiven for the past so you can forgive your kids in the future.

In relationship to your children: Tell your family about a time you really felt forgiven, a time when you felt free to "come home." What did it feel like? What did it do to your relationship with your parents?

STEP ONE

In relationship to God: Pray that God will help you focus on the rules your family needs right now.

In relationship to your children: Design a "rules of the house" card. List your five most important rules and make sure everyone gets a copy to put in his or her room. Post one copy on the refrigerator or family bulletin board.

Chapter Seven

KIDS NEVER FORGET CRISIS TIMES

S cott found his pet fish floating upside down in the fish-bowl. It definitely had been a very bad day for the fish, and Scott was devastated. He ran into the kitchen, fish in hand, and announced through his tears, "Henry's dead!"

Scott's quick-thinking mom took one look at the motionless fish and decided this was a great opportunity to teach a lesson about life and death.

"Oh, Scott, I'm so sorry," she offered. "Take Henry outside, and I'll help you bury him in the flower bed by the garage."

Scott took his sadness and his lifeless fish outside, while Mom grabbed an empty matchbox and a hand shovel and joined him on the grass. Mom placed Henry into the little "coffin" matchbox and talked to Scott about the cycle of life.

Scott talked about how much he would miss Henry, and then Mom and Scott dug a little grave just the right size for the matchbox. Just as Scott picked up the "coffin" to place it in the little grave, Henry began flipping around!

"Wow, Scott," Mom exclaimed. "Henry's still alive. Isn't that great!"

"Yeh," Scott replied. "Let's kill him!"

Scott's grief was overshadowed by the new experience of a burial ceremony. He was enjoying Henry's burial service so much he didn't want it to stop. Don't you wish real-life, adult crises were as easy to deal with?

When children are defeated in an election, are betrayed by a friend, or lose a pet, it's crisis time. At the baseline, all crises are the same. Good or bad, each crisis we face requires more personal resources from us than we have available at the moment. As parents, our first reaction to children in crisis is to solve the problem, heal the hurt, and rescue them from danger, but if we do that at every crisis, our children will never grow up. They will never get the chance to work through the crisis and to find the deeper understanding of life that always waits on the other side.

As parents, our most effective role in helping our kids face crisis times is that of a coach. We train them in the basics and give them a game plan, but they have to play the game. One of our fundamental tasks as a crisis coach is to get our children to share their crisis. Children need to learn, early on, that it's helpful to share their crisis-feelings, preferably with someone who has more resources. As their coach through crises, we can help them come out on the other side with more wisdom and more resources for handling future crises.

P R I N C I P L E

*Children need parents
who will coach them through crises,
not rescue them.*

CHILDREN DON'T HAVE TO BE TOLD ABOUT CRISES

Within the first few weeks of Bill Clinton's presidency, ABC produced a Saturday children's special. Children from across America were given the chance to ask the president their questions. Peter Jennings served as the moderator.

As I watched the media event, it was obvious that most of the questions had been scripted. Some were fun and some were serious. But then Elizabeth surprised them with an unscripted question. Elizabeth was from northern California, and her father was out of work because of the controversy over preserving the spotted owl. She pulled out her school's yearbook and showed the president all the children whose parents had lost their jobs due to the controversy.

They didn't have to script Elizabeth's question. Our kids are more aware of the world around them than we realize. They worry daily about drugs, guns, gangs, AIDS, the environment, and unemployment. They live with crisis every day.

Many of them have misplaced the fun of childhood while concerning themselves with adult-sized problems. These kids need desperately to talk to someone who has more resources than they. If they don't get help, they may burden themselves prematurely with problems that they don't have the resources yet to understand.

P R I N C I P L E

*Parents need to be sensitive
to the worries children may be wrestling with,
and children need to talk about them.*

After many interviews with kids and adults, I have concluded that the greater the level of the child's fear, the more intense the crisis and the more lasting the memory. Fear is one of the first crises children face, and during those fearful times they really need a coach.

Childhood Fears

Fear is a natural and necessary part of childhood. Without it, a child cannot develop emotionally. Conquering childhood fears is a mark of growth and maturity for our kids. Haven't you heard a youngster say, "Well, I used to be afraid of the dark, when I was little, but now I'm big"?

Alfred Hitchcock's father purposefully set up a terrifying experience for his son. When Hitchcock was barely five, his father sent him to the police station with a note sealed in an envelope. "Wait there for a reply," his father said.

The young boy ran as fast as he could, and when he arrived at the police station, he handed the envelope to the captain. The police captain read the note and said, "Come with me."

They walked down the long hallway to a vacant cell. The policeman put the boy in the cell, closed the door, and declared, "This is what we do to naughty boys." Then he walked away.

For ten minutes young Hitchcock cried, but no one was there to hear him. Finally, the captain returned, as the note had instructed, and released the boy without saying a word.

Hitchcock ran away as fast as he could. He was totally confused.

That fear stayed with him for the rest of his life. Later Hitchcock learned how to turn that childhood fear into an uncanny ability to create suspense. He learned how to pass his childhood terror down to generations.

Who knows what was going through his father's mind. But at the very time Alfred needed a coach to help him cope with the normal fears in a young boy's life, his father was adding to those fears.[1]

Fortunately, most parents are more interested in overcoming fears than in creating them. At least this next father had the beginnings of a game plan.

As the thunder and lightning were crashing all around him, a young boy ran to his dad, crying, "Daddy, Daddy, I'm afraid."

Together they walked back into the bedroom and sat down on the bed. The little boy sobbed as he told his dad about the terrible thunder and lightning.

Dad said, "Now, son, remember. Anytime you're afraid, talk to God. Tell him about your fear and about how tough it is, and he will help you with it. Can you do that, son?"

"I think so," the little boy replied.

So they prayed that God would help him with his fear. Everything seemed fine. The little boy snuggled back into bed, and Dad kissed him goodnight and went back to the living room.

As soon as the lightning and thunder struck again, the youngster made a beeline straight for his dad and jumped up into his lap without saying a word.

Dad smiled and said, "I thought you were going to talk to God about this."

The little boy replied, "I know, Dad, but I want somebody with skin on!"

Parents can be a source of fear, causing a crisis,
or they can be a source of strength,
reducing the crisis.

Rejection at School

We moved to a different town just as I entered junior high school. Making the transition from elementary school to junior high is a tough experience for any twelve-year-old, but Mr. Bell made it an ordeal for me.

There were eleven of us "new" kids, and for the first two days we were tested to see if we could fill in the right little bubbles with marks from number two pencils. On the morning of the third day I got my class schedule. My first period was Mr. Bell's English class. By the time I found the right classroom, I was late and scared. I waited outside the door for a few seconds, trying to collect the courage to walk in. Then at the very moment I opened the door, the class erupted in laughter. I knew they were laughing at me. My skinny frame sported thick, horn-rimmed glasses and embarrassing new "tin-grin" braces.

Not daring to look up, I walked over to Mr. Bell with my eyes fixed on his shoes. When I handed him my schedule, he responded, "Oh, no!" My heart stopped in pain. I thought about running away to Australia. Mr. Bell pointed to a chair by the door and said, "Sit there for now. We'll see about getting you a desk tomorrow." Later I realized he reacted as he did because there were no more desks in the room, but the damage was already done.

I sat there reliving those horrible moments. I couldn't wait for the bell to ring. Then I noticed I had Mr. Bell for math and science also. This was a certifiable "terrible, horrible, no good, very bad day."

Eventually things got better—from my perspective they couldn't have gotten worse—but it took a whole year to repair the damage done that day. Ironically, the name of my junior high was Edmond Downer Junior High. For me, the school certainly lived up to its name. I kept the pain and loss of confidence a secret for years. After all, my old grade school buddies were gone forever. I was, in my mind, all by myself—alone.

I needed a crisis coach. I needed a parent who would listen to my feelings without judgment, a parent who could help me devise a plan, a parent who would keep checking with me to see how the plan was working. I thought I was too grown up to go to my mom, and my dad was in the middle of his own crisis with alcohol, so I just stuffed my feelings inside.

P R I N C I P L E

*An effective crisis coach will listen without judgment,
make sure the facts are accurate,
and help the child take action.*

FAMILY CRISES

As our children grow into adolescence, they live for crisis. In fact, if they don't have a crisis working, they will manufacture one because without a crisis brewing, boredom sets in. And the last thing a teen wants to live with is boredom.

Manufactured Crisis

For some teenagers, the most memorable crisis times are the ones they instigated. Patti Davis, daughter of former president Ronald Reagan, remembers the trouble she stirred up: "My mother was embarrassed to be seen with me, with my hair falling over one eye, Veronica Lake style, my overdone make-up, and my tight jeans. And, of course, my attitude—'a chip on the shoulder a mile high'...My father was baffled, uncomfortable with dissension in the ranks....The final blow came when I pulled my hair back, exposed my newly pierced ears, and said, 'Since you're getting upset, you might as well get upset about this, too. I pierced my ears.' My mother seethed, I stood defiant, and my father said, 'Well, before you get your appendix out, do you think you could let us know in advance?'"[2]

Interjecting humor into the crisis can be a welcome and helpful part of the game plan, unless the humor is built on put-downs. Parents who have a healthy sense of humor will help their kids relax, and relaxed people deal with crisis more effectively.

P R I N C I P L E

Humor is an important resource for crisis times.
It helps everyone stay balanced.

Divorce Trauma

Debbie sat across from my desk, picking at the pleats in her skirt, and said, "When my mom and dad divorced, I lost everything. I lost my home, my neighborhood friends, my dreams. I remember the last big fight. I can remember everything about that evening. I felt like I was being left, like it was my fault. I felt that I had done something that caused them to be mad at each other."

The following comments are from kids who have faced the trauma of a divorce-torn home. Their words are like snapshots of the pain. They don't tell the whole story, but they help us get a picture of the devastation that divorce wrecks, not only on the spouses, but on the children.

"Dad said divorce would be a cure, but this feels more like a disease," Becki said.

Gary added, "Divorce is a process that never ends. Never! It's not a solution; it's more like a swap shop."

"Divorce is like a big black cloud," Jennifer offered, "a cloud that keeps growing bigger and bigger until it bursts and puts a hole in your heart."

Corey said, "Divorce is like two lions in a den attacking each other. All kids can do is sit behind a window and watch them kill each other."

Elli's parents divorced several years ago, but she vividly remembers *the* day. "I came downstairs, and Mom said, 'Dad left last night.' I just went 'Huh?' I thought I was in some kind of nightmare. The next day my dad picked me up from school and talked to me. He said 'I don't love your mother anymore.' I didn't know what to say. I just looked at him and thought, Who are you? He seemed like someone else. A month later I found out about the other women. I'll never forget those days."

Divorce is potentially the most difficult loss experience children will ever face—even worse than death—because it shatters the security and trust of their world. It is the only socially acceptable form of child abuse in this country.

P R I N C I P L E

Don't assume everything's fine
when children seem to be coping.
All children can benefit from sharing their feelings
and their pain.

Death of a Friend

I had fallen asleep as a passenger in a car full of college students headed home for Christmas, and I awoke as a patient in

St. Joseph's Hospital in Phoenix, Arizona. A nurse brought me a newspaper clipping about the accident. Tim, my college roommate and childhood friend, was dead. And I was halfway between college and home, alone in a sterile, pale green hospital room.

I was in stable condition with fifty-eight stitches in my face—and lots of time to think.

Tim had avoided the head-on collision, but at seventy m.p.h. he lost control of the car, and we did backflips into the desert. He was killed instantly. I was thrown clear.

I could see Tim's face; I could hear his last words just before I fell asleep: "This is going to be the best Christmas ever. I can't wait!"

Three days later, sore and bandaged, I sat at the funeral. Hundreds of teenagers from all over northern California were there. Tim's zest for life was contagious, and his attitude and sense of humor were unforgettable.

That tragic week just before Christmas 1966 changed my life forever. I grieved for months. I wondered why I was still alive. I got serious about my relationship with God. And I discovered a new relationship with my parents. Perhaps because there was no way they could rescue me from the pain of the moment, they prayed and gave me time and space to heal.

That Christmas initiated me into adulthood.

Grief is always a mixture of feelings. Tell your children about your feelings and ask what's on their mind. Don't wait for them to ask questions. Some children will never ask. Give them time to think. Don't try to distract or cheer them up. It's more helpful to say, "I can see you're worried, and that's okay."

People handle grief differently. Some treasure time alone. Others want to talk all the time. Many find it helps to write out their thoughts, and some cry all the time. Many are helped by reading or being read to, while a few find doing things for others is the only way through the pain. Some children are so overwhelmed by worry or sadness that their emotions freeze or reverse into giddiness.

Grieving children may feel there is something wrong with them if they are unable to cry or feel the same way as others are feeling. Remember, there's no one way to react. The parent's task is to accept the feelings, share any similar feelings, and resist the urge to try to fix it. As crisis coaches, we are called to care, not to cure.

P R I N C I P L E

Children need to know that there is nothing too sad or too terrible to be talked about, written about, or prayed about.

Death of a Sibling

When James Barrie was six years old, his older brother died. His mother was so consumed by the loss that her grief extended into a tormented depression.

In order to comfort her, James pretended to be his brother. He wore his brother's clothes, learned to whistle like his brother, and determined to stay thirteen forever. His mother convinced him that "to be a child was to be free from sorrow," so as James grew older, he tried to capture youth as a defense against tragedy.

Some would say that James Barrie never grew up. Later in life, recalling his own unusual childhood, he wrote the classic adventure of Peter Pan and Never-Never Land, where little boys stay little boys.

James Barrie never forgot his mother's words. In fact he wrote *the* book on it.

The loss of a sibling hits close to home and intensifies a child's fear. Children who are dealing with the death of a sibling need parents who will talk openly about the loss and who will answer questions, regardless of what they are. This is a time to help your child commemorate the life of the one who has died, not to try to take that person's place.[3]

P R I N C I P L E

Effective crisis coaches seek help
when they get beyond their own resources.
Getting help is a sign of strength, not weakness.

Loss of Innocence

According to Claudia Black, pioneer therapist with children of alcoholics, children from addictive families often feel responsible for, and even defensive of, the parent's addiction. The children of alcoholics, for example, will do everything they can to hide their situation and their pain. In the process, the innocence of childhood disappears. Black illustrates this point with the story of Michael.

Michael is one of the brightest kids in class, a teacher's pet, and one of the best behaved kids in school. In fact his teacher often uses him as an example of good behavior—"Why can't we all be like Michael?" Michael has learned to stay quiet.

Each day after school Michael waits at the corner for his mother to pick him up. This is always the hardest moment of the day. What will she look like? How will she sound? He can tell immediately if she's been drinking.

He waits. She's fifteen minutes late. If she has been drinking, Michael will have to cook dinner and straighten up the house.

He will search for the alcohol and pour it down the drain so no one will know.

She has never been thirty minutes late before. The biggest problem at home is during vacation time. He would like to play with his friends, but he is afraid to bring them home. He is afraid to go out and play, too, because then she will drink. Michael wouldn't want to be blamed for that. So he stays in and reads. He doesn't tell his friends; he just holds it in.

After forty-five minutes Michael decides to walk the ten blocks home. After all, he has dinner to fix and his sister to care for. He is the responsible one. He never complains. He never argues, never yells. He is the best little boy in the world.

When he gets home, he can't find his mom. Finally, in the closet in his own bedroom, he sees her dressed in her slip, sitting with a belt tied around her neck and attached to the wooden rod, sobbing. She has been drinking. But Michael wouldn't tell anyone, ever. He will hold it in.[4]

Without some help, Michael will live his life feeling responsible for everybody's life but his own. All his attention will be given to assuming responsibility for his mother, and his life will be absorbed in hers. With help, though, Michael can break the cycle and discover his life as it was meant to be lived. Help can come from a parent who gets help and deals with the addiction problem, or from a parent who forces the child to pour out all the feelings and fears that have been buried deep inside.

PRINCIPLE

Children raised with an alcoholic parent grow up
in constant fear of abandonment.
They need to get their anger out
before it becomes bitterness.

Surrounded by Violence

In April 1993 the *Fort Worth Star-Telegram* ran an investigative series on children and violence in Tarrant County, Texas. The paper reported that a large number of local youngsters say they have to watch their backs. Violence and crime are routine in their neighborhoods and schools.

Greg, a thirteen-year-old, has been jabbed in the side with a compass, hit with a wooden bench in the locker room, hand-cuffed to a school bus seat, shoved and taunted and kicked until he has gone home with bruises on his shins. "There's not a whole lot you can do to stop it, but you can avoid it," he says. Greg never goes to the bathroom at school. None of his friends do. That's where kids get jumped.

Billy, fourteen, carries a scar on his forehead because he walked across the street to watch a gang fight and was shot.

Reggie, sixteen, says, "You can't walk nowhere, you can't wear certain colors, you can't do anything without getting threatened. I'm constantly being scared."[5]

In August 1993 *Time* reported on kids and their guns in Omaha, Nebraska. One young man interviewed for the article stated, "If you have a gun, you have power. Guns are just a part of growing up these days....Parents just don't understand that everything has changed. You can't just slug it out in the schoolyard anymore and be done with it. Whoever loses can just get a gun."

In four months this young man participated in nine drive-by shootings. His targets were cars and houses, and although he says he was not aiming at anybody, there have been some near misses.[6]

You don't have to live in L.A. or Fort Worth or Omaha to have children living in constant fear of violence, guns, and drive-by shootings. One of my daughter's friends was shot in the shoulder last week as he walked out of a convenience store. The closer it gets to home, the scarier it is.

What can we do? Crisis coaches will get involved in the lives of their children. They will encourage their children to talk about their fears, and they will make their home a nonviolent, safe house. They will try to understand the teenage search for power, and they will band together with other concerned parents to deal with the root causes of the violence in their community.

P R I N C I P L E

When kids don't have crisis coaches,
they find their own way of dealing with crisis times.
Left to themselves,·
they will often make unwise choices.

Surprised by Disaster

In a natural disaster the physical debris eventually gets hauled away, but the images and feelings litter our children's memories for years.

In 1928, almost without warning, a monstrous hurricane slashed Miami and the Florida coast. Lucinda, Charles, and their three children stood at the door of the cabin and knew danger was on its way. The nine-foot mud dike around Lake Okeechobee suddenly broke, and water began to surge all around them. Then the hurricane blew off the roof of their cabin.

The family of five struggled through the rising floodwaters and climbed up into the old bent tree just a few feet from the house. As the water level rose, they climbed higher until finally they were clinging to the top branches. The water continued to rise until it came to the adults' shoulders. Charles and Lucinda had to hold the children up so their faces were above the water.

Charles began to predict their death, but Lucinda kept telling him to pray and trust God. "The Lord is here with us. You just hold up those children," she said. They prayed, and sang, and survived. Early in the morning the wind calmed and the rain stopped. By noontime the next day, the water had receded enough for them to get out of the tree. They were battered, hungry, and tired, but they were alive.[7]

In the midst of that crisis the children were held secure and lifted up by their parents' strong hands and their mother's forceful words.

<hr>

P R I N C I P L E

Surviving a disaster together as a family builds intense memories and strong family loyalty.

WHERE DO WE BEGIN?

In his book *Children and Stress*, Arnold Burron tells about a family secret that helped one family survive numerous financially tough times. While many of the kids at school worried when their dads lost their jobs or when they had to do without, this family had a secret.

One of the kids remembered, "I was never really concerned because I was in on a family secret—the jar."

This young man's father had taken him and his sister into the basement and gently loosened a stone. He reached behind that stone and pulled out a plain, old, glass jar filled with coins and paper money. He explained to them that when he had a little extra money, he would put it into the jar, and when they really needed more money for something, he would take money from the jar. He told them they were never to touch it nor to tell anyone about it. He just wanted them to know it was there. He said, "If anything ever happens to me, you remind mom about where it is."

The times stayed tough for a number of years. But the kids never seemed to worry, because when a crisis would hit, Dad would say, "Well, I suppose I'll have to go to the jar."

No one ever disturbed the stone or the jar. The kids never even talked about it, but they were glad it was there.

Years later, when times were better, their mom shared the real secret of the jar. It seems that at the most crucial times there was not more than a few dollars in Dad's jar.

"It was Dad's quiet confidence that dispelled our worries. That was the real treasure of the jar."[8]

Giving your children a quiet sense of confidence during the crisis times is a critical first step for all families.

P R I N C I P L E

*Parents set the crisis climate within the home,
whether they realize it or not.
Children need to see parents' confidence in God in action.*

Personal Crises

In relationship to God: Pray that God will help you not to be the cause of your children's crises but their source of strength in crises.

In relationship to your children: Learn the art of meandering conversation. When you're working a puzzle with your kids or riding in the car together, talk about worries or other crisis times. As a way to get started, use something you heard about, something you saw on TV, or something that happened to you as a child.

Family Crises

In relationship to God: Pray that God will help your children learn to share their feelings with you and that you will be aware when they need you.

In relationship to your children: Plan a Parent Promise Time. Prepare a parental vow that you will read to your children. In your statement, promise them you will love them, that you will be there when they need you, that you will listen to their hurts, that you will be the best you can be, and that you will help them to be the best they can be. The more secure your children are, the more willing they will be to share their crisis times with you.

Sign your statement/vow and give each child a copy to keep.

Community Crises

In relationship to God: Ask God to prepare you to handle the unforeseen crises you may face in the future. Trust his promise that he will always be with you.

In relationship to your children: While you are trapped in one of those traffic tie-ups, or you're waiting in line at the store, or you're quietly drinking a cup of coffee early in the morning, daydream about how you would react in a disaster. Where would you turn for help? How would you help your kids? What would you take with you in a fire or flood? What sacrifices would you make? What would be the most difficult thing to deal with?

These self-awareness trips can serve as minipreparation times and can alert you to precautions you need to take.

STEP ONE

In relationship to God: Ask God to help you build an atmosphere of security and serenity in your home.

In relationship to your children: Become a crisis coach for your kids. Listen to their concerns, teach them a game plan, and let them play the game. As they work through their crises, look for ways to demonstrate to your children the confidence you have in God. Make sure your children know you are depending on God and his care.

Chapter Eight

KIDS NEVER FORGET THE TRADITIONS OF HOME

When I was thirty years old, my mother sorted through several old shoeboxes that held the "treasures" of my childhood. She gathered selected odds and ends that she thought I would appreciate and made a scrapbook of my life—the growing up years.

As I turned the pages, the memories overwhelmed me. I remembered stories, sounds, smells, trips, tastes, songs, and people. It was the best gift I've ever received.

The scrapbook contained pieces of my life:

pictures of relatives long gone

school papers and awards

my first tooth given to the tooth fairy

pictures of birthdays, Christmases, and summer vacations

report cards

special scouting projects

pen pal letters and notes I wrote to friends in junior high

pictures of camp

pictures of firsts—first tricycle, first fight with my cousin, first two-wheeler, first barbershop haircut, first car, first girlfriend

wedding pictures

and a collection of pictures I thought I had burned.

The pages took me back to treasured feelings of growing up, and those feelings help me to re-establish my roots in the past—my heritage. If I were to forget those memories, my life would be diminished to a short-lived existence. Because of them, I feel rooted and secure.

FLASHBULB MEMORIES

Flashbulb memories are vivid observations that stick with us for life. The details are frozen in time, just waiting for us to return. These moments from our childhood shape our expectations about what homes and families and growing up are all about, and many of them will be recreated as our children build their adult lives and their own homes.

I asked a large number of college students to describe the memories of their childhood. I was interested in the positive feelings, the good times. The following quotes illustrate how music and art and tastes and smells are tied to the things we remember.

"Mom and Dad went to a Gaither concert, and from then on we listened to Gaither songs—'You're Something Special,' 'You Are a Promise,' 'Because He Lives,' and 'We Have These Moments.'"

"My dad has all the old Peter, Paul, and Mary albums. He sings their songs in the shower."

"We play Christmas songs from the day after Thanksgiving until Christmas Day. It's great!"

"I remember the 'Itsy Bitsy Spider' and camp songs like 'B-I-N-G-O' that we would sing on car trips."

"My mom filled our hallway with family pictures. It was embarrassing. If someone special was coming over, I would take down the pictures I was in."

"The best pictures in our house were the ones on the refrigerator door. It was our art gallery."

"I remember coming home from school and smelling fresh baked cookies as soon as I opened the door. I always went straight home."

"We had popcorn every night. At our house you could always smell either popcorn or coffee."

"I remember waking up to the smell of bacon frying. Whatever happened to bacon?"

"My mom used lots of Pinesol cleaner and Glade air freshener. I don't think she liked the smell of Dad's cigarettes."

"Our septic tank was always giving us problems. I remember that smell real well."

"My dad smoked a pipe when I was young, and every time I smell that pipe tobacco I can see my dad sitting in his recliner."

"Dad used to watch TV all weekend," Johnnie declared. "Then my mom and dad started betting on the games. If Mom won, Dad would have to do whatever she wanted him to do for the rest of the day. If Dad won, Mom had to do what he wanted. I'm not sure what they bet, but they spent a lot of time in their room after the games."

Most flashbulb memories are candid shots. Very few can be staged. Johnnie's parents weren't staging their weekend game for his benefit, but Johnnie was listening and watching and learning. Children who grow up in families where parents express their love for each other, write notes to each other, and keep a spirit of playfulness with each other will have lots of flashbulb memories that will shape their expectations about marriage, family, and the future. These candid shots are an important part of the legacy all parents pass down to their children.

PRINCIPLE

With our children taking snapshot memories at random,
it doesn't mean our homes
and marriages have to be perfect.
It means we have to show our kids how to be imperfect
and in love with each other.

CELEBRATION RITUALS

Rituals are the building blocks of traditions. They are not just habits or regular chores. Rituals have symbolic content and provide meaning for the people involved. They keep our family foundations strong by inherently passing on our values from generation to generation.

In families with severe problems, rituals can even be protective. Problem families usually do not openly share their feelings, but they may keep several family rituals. And these rituals become part of the glue that holds a fragmented family together.

Regardless of how strong or weak our family is, rituals help identify us as a unique group of people. Our rituals define how we do family. Just ask any group "What is the right way to celebrate Christmas?" to quickly discover a wealth of family distinctives. Establishing rituals around common celebrations is a good place to begin enhancing your family's traditions.

Birthdays

When our girls were little, birthdays were story days. We began when Julie, our older daughter, was five years old. I gathered all the photographs and slides we had taken of her and organized them into a picture-story of her life. She learned about her birth, our move, her struggles with illness, her first steps, her friends, her relatives, and lots of trips and picnics. Then we talked about what her mother and I hoped her life would be like. It was the story of her life—past, present, and future—and it became our birthday ritual.

Now a young woman, Julie still likes to hear her story, and she thinks she remembers coming home from the hospital two days after her birth.

P R I N C I P L E

Whatever else you do, develop birthday rituals.
They are indispensable in helping families celebrate life
and love and each person's unique gift to the family.

Thanksgiving

Cheryl, now twenty-two, told me, "As our family gathered around the Thanksgiving table, each person had to tell about some person and some event for which he or she was thankful. The first person, Grandma Roberts, said, 'I'm thankful for good health.' The next person, Grandpa Roberts, said, 'I'm thankful for Grandma's good health and my new job at WalMart.' Even our guests had to participate. Then, as we all held hands, Daddy led the prayer."

"Every year at our house," Carl remembered, "Grandpa or Grandma told what Thanksgiving was like when they were kids. One year my dad recorded the story on videotape, but until Grandpa and Grandma died, they still told their story live. I'm really glad we did that each year."

Winston grew up in a family with seven brothers and sisters. One week before Thanksgiving 1975 he got a great idea to surprise his parents. He asked all his brothers and sisters to write about why they were thankful to be a member of the family. Then they shared the essays with their parents on Thanksgiving Day. The result was the beginning of the "Reese Family Treasures," a collection of funny stories, wholesome memories, essays, and photographs of the family "authors." Over the years the contributions have ranged from one-page essays to an eight-page play. Now as the children grow up and start their own families, the "Reese Family Treasures" is updated with material from the newest members of the family. What a great ritual!

PRINCIPLE

The Thanksgiving ritual is a natural opportunity to thank God for his care and to celebrate the family heritage and blessings.

Christmas

When did you open gifts—Christmas Eve or Christmas morning? Was your tree real or artificial? What did you do with your socks—wear them or hang them? The Christmas holidays have probably given rise to more disagreements among newlyweds than any other event of the year. However you celebrate it, it will likely be one of the top traditions in your family.

Randy recalled the twelve days of Christmas at his house. During the first week of December they drew names for secret pals in the family. Starting twelve days before Christmas, they each did something nice for their secret pal. Then, on Christmas Eve at dinner, they tried to guess who was their secret pal and thank him or her.

Each of our girls gets her own tree ornament every year, which certainly has given our tree an eclectic flare through the years. When the girls leave home, the ornaments are theirs to take with them, along with the memories.

Dustin, a young man from Denver, told me about his fun-loving father. "It was a ritual for my dad to do something crazy each Christmas. One Christmas he bought a fifteen-foot Christmas tree and cut off the top. After positioning the bottom of the tree in front of our big picture window, he climbed up on the roof and tied the top of the tree directly in line with the bottom. Then he strung the lights in exactly the same way on the top and the bottom, making it look like we had cut a hole in our roof to get the tree in. Was that crazy or what? I loved it."

Donald Davis, freelance writer, claims his most unforgettable Christmas was not the year Freddie Patton tried to stop Joe-brother's nosebleed with his bicycle pump, and it wasn't the year that Miss Swineburne ate the cookies that had soaked up fumes from the airplane glue used to decorate the inside of the cookie box. It was the year he learned about Santa Claus.

I was ten years old and Joe-brother was nine, and we both wanted scooters and our only hope was Santa.

I decided not to take any chances with Santa so I told him at Belk's department store and again at Harris department store. Before the season was over I talked to him twenty-seven times.

The day before Christmas we pulled into Jimmy's Drive-In Restaurant. When Jimmy came with the food, he carried four Cokes with the bottlenecks between his fingers. Jimmy said, "You got any bottles to swap?"

We always had empties in the trunk. So, I tore around the car to get them. I heard Mother and Daddy gasp. You didn't need a key to open the trunk, just turn the handle, and I did. There before my eyes were two brand-new red scooters. I slammed the trunk as fast as I could. "No bottles!" I blurted as I climbed back into the car. I never said a word to Joe-brother.

Christmas morning came and after we had opened all our presents Daddy said, "Your mother and I were awful worried. We knew you had been asking Santa for scooters, but we were afraid that Santa would never get them down the chimney. So, your mother and I decided to buy you the scooters ourselves. We've had them hidden in the car. You can get them if you want to."

Late that night, Joe-brother and I decided that after this year it didn't matter what the other kids said about Santa Claus because, at best, he only came around once a year anyway. But our Mother and Daddy, well, we had them all the time.[1]

PRINCIPLE

Any celebrations of Christmas that focus a family on the spirit of the season are worth keeping.

"THE WAY WE DID IT" RITUALS

Every family has a host of rituals that aren't connected to birthdays, Thanksgiving, or Christmas; they are woven into the fabric of everyday life. These distinctive, nonholiday rituals help parents build a healthy family identity throughout the year.

Rock Brynner remembers the ritual he and his father, Yul Brynner, shared: "No matter how much of a nightlife he was living, he maintained our ritual of early breakfast....We read the paper together (even before I could really read), watched Dave Garroway, and savored the morning as the familiar wake-up smells of coffee, cigarettes and grilled sirloin made the day begin. All this transpired without a word between us. The rest of the day might have been filled with conversation, but breakfast was a sacred, silent ritual, a building block in the larger lesson Yul was trying to teach his son: the value of rituals."[2]

Breaking Out the Candles

I remember a number of times when our electricity would go off because of bad weather. Regardless of what everyone was doing before the power outage, when the lights went out, we all knew what to do. Mom would get the candles, I would get the Chinese Checkers board, and if Dad was home, he would get the card table. We set everything up by the window and played till the lights came back on. Rather than being afraid or upset I was excited. Sometimes I wished our electricity would go off more.

Mom's Journal

Pam said her mom wrote everything down. "When we went on trips, Mom wrote about what we saw and what we did and what everyone thought about the day. Mom took her journal with her everywhere; she would write in it at the grocery store, in restaurants, at church, and at soccer games. When she finished a journal, she stored it with the others in a trunk in the attic. She calls that truck her 'memory management system.' On special wintry days Mom would let us get into the chest and read her journals. It was better than anything on TV."

Losing the First Tooth

The first tooth I lost was a tough one. I could move it back and forth with my tongue, but it just wouldn't turn loose. My dad tied a piece of string around the tooth, and while he was kidding about tying the other end of the string to the doorknob, he pulled the tooth out, and I didn't even feel it. I went running into the kitchen proudly displaying my liberated tooth still connected to the string. In fact that night I slept with the tooth and string tucked under my pillow. The tooth fairy visited me that night, trading my tooth and string for fifty cents. I loved getting the money, but I never understood why anyone or anything would want to collect old teeth.

Saturday Bath

Andy Tickner wasn't very big, but he talked a lot. When he found out I took a bath every Saturday night, he predicted I would die from soaking up too much water. He said that if a person took too many baths his body would dissolve so I shouldn't use up my number of baths in the third grade. It made sense to me, but my mom said Andy was a numskull. From that moment on, I decided not to tell Mom about the other theories I was working on. And whether Andy Tickner was right or not, I still had to take a bath every Saturday night.

Vacations

When I asked a gathering of teens in Dallas to recall their most positive memories of childhood, the overwhelming response was family trips. It really didn't matter what they did or how much it cost. It was the shared time that was important. Vacation trips put everybody on the same schedule. They give us the opportunity to spend concentrated time together, to eat all our meals together, and to get tired together.

I remember one of our vacation trips vividly. My sister, LaJuana, my brother, Gary, and I rode from Richmond,

California, to Harrison, Arkansas, fighting for position in the back seat of our 1955 Ford. I learned a lot on that trip. I discovered that outhouses and wasp nests go together, that ticks and chiggers love city kids, and that you shouldn't try to throw up out the window while going sixty-five miles an hour.

April Fool's Day

In *Building Happy Memories and Family Traditions*, Verna Birkey and Jeanette Turnquist tell of a young mother who developed a ritual of putting a surprise in her husband's lunch each April Fool's Day. "When our first child started school," she said, "he wanted to be sure I would pack his lunch on April 1, instead of his buying a lunch. I knew he was hoping I would do some of the same special surprises I had done with his daddy. When he was in first grade, I packed his lunch on April 1. Instead of the usual one sandwich, I put in two. The top one had cardboard between a buttered roll; the next one was his favorite baloney. He was delighted that I also remembered him with a little amusing trick."[3]

Parents' Day

Since 1911, when Anna Jarvis led the effort to establish Mother's Day as a national observance, the most common celebration of this day has become eating out. More people eat out on Mother's Day than any other day of the year. Although Father's Day didn't become official until 1972, it has continued to develop its own rituals, like the buying of ties. Both days are important family days because they encourage us to build rituals around them

Just before these special days, millions of children get construction paper, crayons, scissors, pictures, and other assorted creative materials and make their own cards. These treasured, homemade cards are collected, displayed on the refrigerator or family bulletin board, and finally stored away in boxes in closets or attics for safekeeping. But the real power of these special days is not found in the cards. It's found in training children to honor their parents. Our example is our best training method here. As parents honor their own parents and each other, the children are taught to honor and to give back to the adults in their family.

School's Out

In southern California, Howard shared that for ten years his family has done the same thing on the first Saturday of summer vacation. "Starting early on that Saturday morning we all gather in the garage and clean it out together. Then we cook hot dogs on the grill. When we started, it was tough for the children to do much, but through the years they have learned to really help. As a kid, I remember the family joining forces to clean out the basement once a year, and I wanted my family to grow up with the same kind of experience. Plus, with everybody working we get the job done much faster."

Bedtime Prayer

"We had a special bedtime routine," Sonya reported. "Each night we got two cookies and a glass of milk, brushed our teeth, got our pajamas on, and then everyone in the family sat in a circle on the bed for prayer time. We held hands, and each one said part of the prayer. Dad would finish it, and we would sing 'Jesus Is Lord.' As we grew older, we got to read for a while, but we never missed our prayer time. I still pray every night when I go to bed."

Exercise Night

A preacher friend of mine from Miami, Florida, told me about his family exercise ritual. Once a week, this young family spends about thirty minutes exercising together. They all jump rope together, sometimes quoting Bible verses as they jump.

Sometimes they play catch with different types of balls. At other times they take a walk together. At least one of their activities is designed to be a little crazy. For example, sometimes each person has to pick up as many marbles as he can within sixty seconds. The trick is, they have to pick up the marbles with their toes.

P R I N C I P L E

*Every family can develop rituals that provide continuity,
fun, common experiences, and memories
that will have value far beyond
the experiences themselves.*

Reunions

Mike, a friend from Fort Worth, just returned from his thirty-year high school reunion. Over half of his graduating class was there. "It was fascinating," Mike said. "They all wanted, in some small way, to relive a moment in time, to reclaim a feeling of youth." All reunions are an attempt to reclaim the best of the past. They help us put all the pieces together—people, places, stories, and feelings.

For adults family reunions help us remember our roots. Even if we don't care much for our "unusual" relatives, we do share kinship. Without family reunions, that kinship fades and we lose a valuable resource. As we grow older, the reunion increases in value.

P R I N C I P L E

*Reunions connect children to their extended family
and reinforce their sense of belonging.*

One tradition I would encourage every mother and father to include in their daily routine is that of blessing their children. As parents, we have daily opportunities to bless or blame our children. Each day we do things or say things that help them feel loved and appreciated, or unloved and unappreciated. A parent's blessing can be informal and unplanned, but deliberate and consistent blessings can have tremendous impact.

Some parents repeat the same blessing each night, usually at bedtime. Some quote a passage of Scripture like Numbers 6:24-26. Others, taking their lead from Jesus, pick up their children and bless them with their own words. To be most effective, the blessing needs to be repeated often, daily if possible.

Gary Smalley and John Trent describe the parental blessing as a process with five elements.

1. Touch, hold, and/or hug your child as you speak.

2. Speak words of encouragement and appreciation: "I love the way you…"

3. Use word pictures that place high value on the person being blessed: "You are like…"

4. Share a special vision of the child's future: "I can see great things like___ in your future."

5. Commit the child to the Lord: "May God give you…"[4]

Blending these five simple elements, a parent can develop his or her own style of blessing, both for formal and informal blessings.

In *The Family Blessing*, Rolf Garborg shares the comments of his children who grew up being blessed. His daughter Lisa said, "Dad, I will never forget the night you blessed me thirty-two times before you left on a trip for that many days. I know that was going a little overboard on my part and probably not necessary, but at the time it put me at ease....One other thing that really stands out is the time you made a tape recording before you left on an overseas trip so we could play it every night you were gone. It was so sweet and contained words of affirmation and encouragement, a prayer for God's protection, and then a blessing for Mom, Carlton and me. All of these special times will stick with me forever."[5]

Another youngster named Kristi reported, "When I was little, my parents blessed me every night....The blessing was sort of like a hug to my head. If I had friends over, my parents would bless them, too....I also made them bless my dog. He was as special as my friends. Sometimes after I had been blessed and tucked in, I would bless my dog as if he were my own child."[6]

As I described the feelings of security, belonging, and affirmation that come from being blessed, dinnertime came to Brenda's mind. "When I was growing up, we couldn't wait for dinnertime," she shared. "No matter how bad a day you'd had, by the time dinner was over, you felt great. All my friends liked to eat at my house, because dinnertime was like a party, only better. Momma was the one who made it happen. She hugged everyone, we talked about the events of the day, and then she thanked God for each of us by name. We ate and ıoked and told stories. I'll never forget those times."

PRINCIPLE

Blessing children on a regular basis builds secure and self-confident youngsters.

Don't assume that if you don't blame your kids, you have blessed them. Words of appreciation, touches of love, catching your kids doing things right, seeing something good when everything looks bad, giving a formal blessing, and providing your kids with a vision of their future takes a conscious effort on your part. Blessing doesn't happen accidentally.

Flashbulb memories, rituals, and blessings give children a healthy sense of family tradition. Taken together they help a family become more aware of its character, its personality, and its heritage. Children who grow up with traditions know what they stand for.

WHERE DO WE BEGIN?

Claim dinnertime as a family tradition. It can be the place for flashbulb memories, blessings, and rituals of all kinds.

Robert and Janese, longtime friends of ours, begin each dinner with the family holding hands and saying grace. Then Robert and Janese kiss and say, "I love you." They have been doing that prior to every meal for seventeen years.

Thomas Lickona, author of *Raising Good Children*, suggests that you can make a game of dinnertime conversation. He describes one possibility: "During the week, each family member cut out a picture from the newspaper and posted it on the refrigerator. On Friday, everybody brought his or her clipping to the table, and the rest of the family tried to guess who was in the picture and what it was about. That was the springboard for further discussion of people and events in the news."[7]

Mealtime is a wonderful first step that everyone will enjoy. If you can only have one family dinner per week, then start there. Just start somewhere!

Flashbulb Memories

In relationship to God: Pray that God will open your eyes to see what your children see. Ask God to help you see the flashbulbs going off.

In relationship to your children: Take lots of pictures. One of the most underrated tools of parenting is the camera. When the pictures are developed, display them where everyone can see them. If you take enough, you are bound to record some of your children's flashbulb memories.

Celebration Rituals

In relationship to God: Pray that God will help you start a new ritual that will be meaningful to everyone.

In relationship to your children: Start a new ritual this year. Decide on two or three possibilities, try them, and then ask the family which, if any, should become one of your annual celebrations.

"The Way We Did It" Rituals

In relationship to God: Ask God to help you discern the rituals that need to be changed and the ones that don't.

In relationship to your children: Make a list of your "way we did it" rituals. Ask your kids and your spouse to help you. Then discuss any of the rituals that need to be changed. Most families need to change some rituals as the kids grow. Change what needs to be changed and add what needs to be added.

Receiving the Blessing

In relationship to God: Ask God to give you the sensitivity and discipline needed to be a blessing parent.

In relationship to your children: Commit yourself to becoming a parent who regularly blesses each of your children. Don't worry about doing it right, or messing up, or repeating yourself. Be sure to hold hands, hug, or put your hands on your child's head as you say the words. There is great power in your touch.

STEP ONE

In relationship to God: Ask God to bless your dinnertime conversations.

In relationship to your children: Take charge of your conversations at the dinner table. Ask questions like:

What do you appreciate about each person in this family?

What did you do today that you feel good about?

What is the funniest thing that happened to you this week?

Is there anything you want the family to be praying about?

Chapter Nine

PARENT-SHAPING MEMORIES

The message on the answering machine had been expected for months, but the words still shocked the young preacher. "Call the Medical Center Hospital as soon as possible. Your father's condition is worsening by the hour."

Stephen dialed immediately and talked his way through to the duty nurse, who urged him to get to the hospital quickly. As he hung up the phone, his mind flashed back twenty-five years to a conversation with his father. Stephen's father, a family doctor, had made no secret of pressuring Stephen to go to medical school and join him in a father-son practice, right there in Petaluma. But Stephen had a different dream for his life.

Their perpetual debate went into hyperdrive when Stephen announced his calling to the ministry and his intention to become a preacher. Since that night, their relationship had become guarded, shallow, and sad. In fact, it had been ten years since Stephen had been back to the old home place, the site of his "I'm going to be a preacher" proclamation.

Stephen's little church in Fresno, less than five hours from Petaluma, kept him too busy for the trip home, he reasoned. He had learned to bury himself in his ministry to others, sacrificing himself as a way of hiding from the truth. The truth was, Stephen felt unloved and devalued by his dad, and that pain was unbearable. So he had decided years ago just to coexist with his dad when necessary, rather than deal with the growing sense of alienation and emotional abandonment.

Stephen's drive to Petaluma was punctuated with little monologues, as though his dad were right there in the car. "Dad, why did I always have to do what you wanted? You never asked me what I wanted." "Why couldn't you love me just the way I am?" "I feel so cheated, so unaccepted. Why, Dad, why?" "You don't even know me, do you, Dad?"

Finally, as he took the off-ramp to the hospital, Stephen asked that quintessential question that every child wants his parents to answer: "Are you proud of me?"

It was shortly after 4:00 A.M. when he arrived, and Stephen was able to move quickly into the hospital and up to room 217. He opened the door, startling the nurse who was taking his dad's blood pressure. She grabbed Stephen's hand and pulled him around the end of the bed. Without saying a word, she placed Stephen's hands on his father's hands.

"Dr. Martin, Dr. Martin, your son's here," she said with a smile. The patient was weak and near death, but those were the words he had been waiting to hear. It was as though he had been willing himself to live until he heard those words.

Once their eyes made contact, nothing else existed—just two generations trying to pack a lifetime into a moment. Stephen's father used all the strength he had to squeeze Stephen's hand and pull him closer. He wanted to whisper something to him. Stephen leaned forward, hoping he was finally going to hear the words he had longed to hear.

The dying man struggled a moment and then whispered slowly and cautiously, "Stephen, are you proud of me?"

Stephen couldn't believe what he was hearing. His proud, self-confident father needed something from him. Dr. Martin needed to know his son was proud of him.

"Yes, Dad. Yes, I'm proud of you."

Dr. Martin died with a peaceful smile on his face. And Stephen's question was answered without his even asking it.[1]

After you strip away all the glitter and bravado, we all want the same thing—to know that our parents are proud of us. And that is at the heart of what our children want from us.

REFLECTION

Perhaps the stories in this book have caused stories from your own collection of memories to resurface. Perhaps these stories have even helped you gain some new insights about your own life. Kierkegaard was right when he said, "Life is meant to be lived forward and understood backward."

However, people who have unfinished business—unresolved conflicts—with their parents will find it difficult to remember their childhood stories. Reading and reflecting on the things kids never forget will aggravate their vulnerability and sense of loss. And if parents feel robbed of something from their childhood, many times the children will pay the price because the parents will either overindulge their children with whatever they were robbed of, or they will rob their children of the same things. Either way, the children are raised in reaction to the past.

I have in my library a music video that reminds me of the tragedy of unfinished business. The setting is a graveyard on the coastal hills of Scotland. The song is "The Living Years" by Mike and the Mechanics:

We open up a quarrel

Between the present and the past

We only sacrifice the future

It's the bitterness that lasts.[2]

Every generation has to decide how it will handle the past. All the memories of failures and abuses can be either prisons we feel trapped within or foundations we build upon. Life in the prison is cynical and hopeless and filled with excuses. Life on the foundation is filled with freedom, hope, and growth. With a little help, we can choose to start fresh and build our lives on the foundation and not in the prison. We can't change the events of the past, but we can change our perspective on them so that we and our children are connected to the positive legacies and freed from the abuses. I know firsthand.

My father was a church-going alcoholic. He completed only eight years of formal education, but he brought home the paycheck and paid the bills. When he was home, he was either asleep or drunk, or both. He never drank in a bar; he didn't go out drinking with the guys. Instead, he would hide his bottles in a garage cabinet or underneath the front seat of the car.

Once I discovered his secret, I began storing memories full of resentment and anger. By the time I was in high school, I had nothing good to say about the man, and I argued with him constantly. For the first nine years of my adult life, I distanced myself from him and my resentment by staying busy trying to fix others.

In June of 1978 Dad messed up my system; he checked himself into an alcoholic treatment center. Forty-five days later he came out of that center, never to drink again. Two and a half years later, on October 29, 1980, he died.

It took eighteen hours for all the family to gather. After we greeted each other and scheduled the funeral service, I slipped out to Dad's workshed. I had to find a way to talk to him and to God.

For over an hour I talked out loud about my fears, my resentment, my pain, my failure, my grief, and my need for forgiveness. When I walked out, my resentment was gone, my burden was lifted, and a new set of memories began replacing the old ones. God locked my resentments within the walls of that workshed, and I was freed to see the good in my father. Finally, I was honored to be my father's son.

I had experienced a cycle-breaking process. I owned my part of the problem—my anger and resentment. I felt the pain and described it and confessed it openly. I gave it to God to heal, and I left it there with him, refusing to take it back. God then opened my memory banks, and new, healthy memories began replacing the old ones.

As a result of making peace with my dad and the past, I found myself more relaxed about being a parent myself. My tension and frustration gradually changed to peacefulness. I felt empowered to accept my kids, warts and all, right where they were. I believe my judgments became more fair and my perspective more balanced. And life took on a new sense of urgency. I wanted to be with my kids, to be more nurturing, to capture the moments, to make as many memories as I could.

This same process of forgiveness will work for you. It's a prerequisite for happiness in families—one that isn't used nearly as much as it is needed.

In the Bible the first command with a promise is to honor our father and mother, but if buried resentment isn't dealt with, we will have trouble keeping the command. Our perspective will force us to see this as a command to our children to honor us, and our relationship with our parents will be ignored. Honoring the person or the memory of the person isn't based on his or her performance; it's based on our gratefulness for the gift of life. We honor our parents for what they have done for us and who they are. And by honoring them, we teach our kids how to honor their parents and grandparents.

The final stanza of "The Living Years" reminds me in a haunting way of both the chain that undeniably links our parents to us and us to our children and our need to make peace with them while there is an opportunity:

I wasn't there that morning

When my father passed away

I didn't get to tell him

All the things I had to say.

I think I caught his spirit

Later that same year

I'm sure I heard his echo

In my baby's new born tears

I just wish I could have told him

In the living years.

May we all make the most of our opportunities with our parents, our spouses, and our children in the living years.

N o t e s

················

Chapter One

1. "We Have These Moments," William J. and Gloria Gaither, © 1975 William J. Gaither. All rights reserved. Used by permission.

2. Arthur Gordon, *Through Many Windows* (Old Tappan, NJ: Fleming H. Revell Company, 1983), 34-6.

Chapter Two

1. Myron Magnet, "The American Family, 1992" *Fortune* (August 10, 1992): 42-47.

2. Robert Munsch and Sheila McGraw, *Love You Forever* (Willowdale, Ontario: Firefly Books Ltd., 1986), 4, 26.

3. Dr. Robert U. Akeret with Daniel Klein, *Family Tales, Family Wisdom* (New York: William Morrow and Company, Inc., 1991), 136.

4. Julius Segal and Herbert Yahraes, *A Child's Journey: Forces that Shape the Lives of Our Young* (New York: McGraw-Hill Book Company, 1978), 287.

5. "Love Without End, Amen," George Straight © 1990 MCA Records, Inc.

6. Charles Swindoll, *Growing Strong in the Seasons of Life* (Portland: Multnomah Press, 1983), 211.

7. Stephen and Janet Bly, *How to Be a Good Grandparent* (Chicago: Moody Press, 1990), 14.

8. Adapted from a story told by Robert Bly on the PBS program *A Gathering of Men.*

9. Helen Mrosla, "All the Good Things," *Reader's Digest* (October 1991): 49-53.

10. Rom. 12:15.

Chapter Three

1. Jim Trelease, *The New Read-Aloud Handbook* (New York: Penguin Books, 1989), xv.

2. Dr. Charles A. Smith, *From Wonder to Wisdom* (New York: Penguin Group, 1989), 6-7.

3. Ibid., 9.

4. Chase Collins, *Tell Me a Story; Creating Bedtime Tales Your Children Will Dream On* (Boston: Houghton Mifflin Company, 1992), 6-7.

5. Ted Koppel, "The Last Word," *AGB Reports* (July/August 1987): 47.

Chapter Four

1. Paul Aurandt, *Destiny*, ed. and comp. Lynne Harvey (New York: William Morrow and Company, Inc., 1983), 242-4.

2. James Sheehy, "You Just Get on It and Go," *Newsweek* (July 30, 1990): 8-9.

3. Adapted from "The Father-Daughter Dance," *McCall's* (June, 1978): 78.

4. Robert L. Veninga, *A Gift of Hope* (New York: Ballantine Books, 1985), 74-75.

5. Charles Colson, "In the Image of Christ," *What My Parents Did Right*, comp. and ed. Gloria Gaither (Nashville: Star Song Publishing Group, 1991), 48.

Chapter Five

1. Barbara Jean Rinkoff, *Rutherford T Finds 21B* (New York: G. P. Putnam's Sons, 1970).

2. Phyllis Reynolds Naylor, *Alice in Rapture, Sort of* (New York: Atheneum Books, 1989), 6-7.

3. David Elkind, *All Grown Up & No Place to Go* (Reading, Mass.: Addison-Wesley Publishing Company, 1984), 45.

4. "Boy, 5, takes kid sister for spin in family car," *Dallas Morning News* (December 5, 1987): 8A.

Chapter Six

1. "Keep It between the Lines," Russell Smith and Kathy Louvin, © 1991 Sony Music Entertainment Inc./"Columbia."

2. Koppel, "The Last Word."

3. "Homeless Couple Return Wallet Containing $2394," Associated Press (March 1, 1993).

4. Garrison Keillor, *Lake Wobegon Days* (New York: Penguin Books, 1985), 332-4.

5. Max Lucado, *No Wonder They Call Him the Savior* (Portland: Multnomah, 1986),157-9.

6. Linda and Richard Eyre, *Teaching Your Children Values* (New York: Simon and Schuster, 1993), 227.

Chapter Seven

1. Paul Aurandt, *More of Paul Harvey's The Rest of the Story*, ed. and comp. Lynne Harvey (New York: William Morrow and Company, Inc., 1980), 141-3.

2. Patti Davis, *The Way I See It* (New York: Putnam Publishing Group, 1992), 69.

3. Aurandt, *More of Paul Harvey*, 241-2.

4. Peter M. Nardi, "The Best Little Boy in the World (He Won't Tell)" *It Will Never Happen to Me!* by Claudia Black (Denver: M.A.C., 1981), 31.

5. Patricia Rodriquez and Mary Gay Johnson, "Scared and Angry," *Fort Worth Star-Telgram* (April 4, 1993): G1-6.

6. Jon D. Hull, "A Boy and His Gun," *Time* (August 2, 1993): 21-7.

7. Norman Vincent Peale, *Favorite Stories of Positive Faith* (Pawling, NY: Foundation for Christian Living, 1974), 56-9.

8. Arnold Burron, *Children and Stress* (Denver: Accent Books, 1988), 53-5.

Chapter Eight

1. Donald Davis, "Who Needs Santa," *Parenting* (December/January, 1993): 38-39.

2. Jon Winokur, comp. and ed., *Fathers* (New York: Dutton Book, 1993), 25.

3. Verna Birkey and Jeanette Turnquist, *Building Happy Memories and Family Traditions* (Old Tappan, NJ: Fleming H. Revell Company, 1980), 40.

4. Gary Smalley and John Trent, *The Blessing*, (Nashville: Thomas Nelson, Inc.,1986), 24.

5. Rolf Garborg, *The Family Blessing* (Dallas: Word, Inc., 1990), 47.

6. Ibid., 50.

7. Thomas Lickona, *Raising Good Children; Helping Your Children through the Stages of Moral Development* (Toronto: Bantam Books, 1983), 259-60.

Chapter Nine

1. Anonymous author

2. "The Living Years," Mike Rutherford/B.A. Robertson, © 1988 Michael Rutherford Ltd./R & BA Music Ltd./Hit & Run Music (Publishing) Ltd. Administered by Hidden Pun Music, Inc. (BMI) for USA. International copyright secured. All rights reserved.